Praise for Sanaya's

"I have to let you know how much I love the writings of Sanaya. It's like they were written just for me...all the lessons I need to work on."
—*B. King, Saginaw, MI*

"I really do believe that 'when the student is ready, the teacher will come,' and Sanaya is the perfect teacher for me at this point in my journey. When I read the daily words, they ring so true for me. I find myself reading them a second time and a third time and can actually feel the vibration of 'knowing.' Thank you, Sanaya and thank you, Suzanne."
—*B. Garlipp, Sodus, NY*

"Sanaya's words are so understandable and provocative. God Bless!"
—*K. Hall, Stoughton, MA*

"I did not really believe that channeling was possible until you. I did not really believe in the spirit world until you. I did not really believe in spirit guides until you, and you have opened up all of these shining possibilities for me. I send you gratitude, admiration and love."
—*L. Mancini, Camp Hill, PA*

"Thanks for the wonderful wisdom you are bringing through from Spirit. What Sanaya says really resonates with me. I am always searching for new sources of wisdom to help me keep moving forward on my spiritual path. So, it's great to have a new daily treat to look forward to, especially one with a perspective that I so closely personally identify with. What you're doing is one of the most important jobs on the planet."
—*C. Lhulier, Boston, MA*

"Thank you, Sanaya, and thank you, Suzanne, for the spirit-filled, love-filled meditations that have inspired me each day of this year. Your teachings have personally touched my soul as if they were meant just for me. You've reminded me to practice the 'art of allowing,' to love unconditionally, to see beauty in All That Is, to live life with gratitude, and to be the love in our world."
—*L. Anderson, Ocala, FL*

Praise for [illegible]

"[illegible] I have [illegible] the writings of [illegible] like they were [illegible] all the lessons I need to [illegible]"

—[illegible]

"[illegible] when [illegible] the reader will [illegible] and [illegible] When I [illegible] [illegible]"

—[illegible]

"[illegible]"

"[illegible]"

—[illegible]

"[illegible]"

—[illegible]

"[illegible]"

—[illegible]

Love Beyond Words

Also by Suzanne Giesemann:

Conquer Your Cravings

Living a Dream

It's Your Boat Too

The Priest and the Medium

Co-Authored with Janet Nohavec:

Through the Darkness

Where Two Worlds Meet

Love Beyond Words

365 Days of Inspiration from Spirit

A *Sanaya Says* collection
compiled by *Suzanne Giesemann*

Published by One Mind Books, www.OneMindBooks.com

Cover and interior design: Elisabeth Giesemann

Interior proofreading: Lois Anne Anderson and Constance England

Library of Congress Control Number: 2011912910

Library of Congress Cataloging-in-Publication Data

Love Beyond Words : 365 Days of Inspiration from Spirit/Suzanne Giesemann

ISBN: 978-0-9838539-0-9

Printed in the United States of America

Preface

Distractions abound these days. Televisions and radios blare at us relentlessly in our homes, in restaurants, and in doctors' waiting rooms. It's hard to find even a few moments of peace. The Internet and cell phones keep us connected with our computers and with each other, but it's far too easy to become disconnected with our *selves*. We rush about "doing," and spend very little time simply "being." Is it any wonder people are stressed out, frustrated, and "looking for love in all the wrong places"?

Throughout the ages, mystics have shared the secrets of spiritual understanding with their disciples. The masters teach that to find peace, happiness, and love, one must spend time in silence and in contemplation. It is then that one discovers another Self beyond the busy human being. It is then that one discovers the true nature of all things. It is then that one discovers the Spirit.

Are you looking for more peace in your life? Are you searching for the happiness that is supposed to be your inalienable right? That is your spirit tugging at your sleeve, trying its best to get your attention. Unfortunately, in this world full of to-do lists, you can have the best intentions to maintain a spiritual practice, but life gets in the way.

That's where the book you hold in your hands will help. Here you'll find a daily dose of spiritual wisdom to place your focus on what matters most … on the things that transcend this transient material world … on the part of you that is eternal … on Spirit.

The 365 entries in this collection come from a spirit-teacher who calls herself Sanaya. I first heard from Sanaya on my birthday. As I sat quietly in meditation, the words flowed easily, and I wrote them down. The first time I heard words in my meditation, one year earlier, I wrote them down, but at the time I chalked the experience up to a vivid imagination.

Thankfully, the spirit world was patient with me. They knew they had to give me clear evidence of whom and what I was dealing with, and I have to give them credit for their brilliance. They did an outstanding job of convincing me that someone other than I was doing the talking. You see, that morning a year earlier, they sent me a poet.

There I sat, quietly focusing on my breath, when I started hearing not just a few words here and there, but one sentence after another. I had pen and paper at my side, so I kept my eyes closed and wrote down the words as fast as they came. The fluency of the phrases was stunning enough, but it was far more than that … these sentences rhymed!

The spirit world knew that I was a published author, but I was certainly no poet. I rarely read poetry and certainly never wrote it. That morning, however, in the space of five minutes, they dictated a three-page poem with a clear and compelling message. The poet minced no words, telling me why the spirit world had been trying to get through to me, and what they expected me to do for them.

Like all good poetry, the final lines summed up the intent of the poem, and I share them with you now:

For we are here; at your side we wait.
It's with great hope we anticipate
The truths you'll carry to those who listen
The truths of God on your words will glisten.

Go now and rest for there's work to do.
We have great love and trust in you.
You have our blessing. In you we're proud.
Take our wisdom and shout it loud.

We love you all. For this we've come.
There is no rest 'til the Spirit's work is done.

Thus began a daily session in which the spirit world dictated their messages to me in rhyme. Any time I would try to fill in my own thoughts, the words stopped.

It was clear who was running the show.

I always wrote with pen and paper in my lap and eyes closed, except for the one time the voice told me to open them and look at the page. When I did, I saw that my pen had run out of ink.

They didn't want me to miss a word.

The poems continued for a year and four days, and after poem #369, they abruptly stopped. I sat for three days with no message from the spirit world, and I have to admit, I felt a bit bereft. Then, on my birthday, a present. As I sat in meditation, a new voice spoke to me. This time the phrases didn't rhyme, but the message was just as beautiful.

By now I knew that I wasn't making up these words. The spirit world had given me a full year of beautiful poetry to shed my skepticism.[1] On that birthday morning, the energy that blended with mine felt both masculine and feminine. I asked this new presence for a name, and the voice told me that "they" were a collective consciousness, and that I was to call them "Sanaya." I later discovered, to my delight, that Sanaya is a female Sanskrit name meaning, "eminent, distinguished, and *of the gods*"—quite a fitting name for a spirit-teacher.

I realize now that Sanaya would not even need a name, except for our human need to put labels on things and place our experiences into well-defined boxes. Sanaya takes us outside the box into a dimension where we come face to face with our higher self. To hear the words of Sanaya as they come through … to sit in that energy … is a palpable experience of higher vibration … of love. To read Sanaya's words can have the same result when you tune in to that finer energy as you read.

Sanaya's teachings, like those of many mystical masters throughout the ages, tell us that there is only One Mind. That Infinite Intelligence to which we are all connected is not readily perceptible while we walk about

---

[1] All 369 poems can be found at www.MessagesOfHopePoems.org

in a waking state. Higher levels of consciousness are, however, accessible to all of us in our dreams, in meditation, and in a waking meditative state. Those higher levels provide us wisdom, guidance, and inspiration when we learn to still the mind and shift our waking consciousness.

The wisdom, guidance, and inspiration that have come through me from Sanaya have changed me. It is impossible to be imbued with this higher energy and to receive these words on a daily basis and not feel more loving, peaceful, and content. And that is what this book holds in store for you. As you read these writings, I ask you to *feel* the words. Take the time to quiet your mind and body before you open to the day's message. Tune into the vibration the message carries as you read it. All writing is imbued with the energy of its author, and Sanaya's words carry a noticeably high vibration.

Here you will read universal truths as Sanaya reminds you of who and what you are: a spirit-being temporarily housed in a body. You will find that she speaks repeatedly of themes such as "oneness" and the nature of God, but always in new and refreshing ways. She even includes a few poems here and there for old times' sake, but whether prose or poetry, the underlying theme is always love.

Sanaya's sayings are like caviar … meant to be savored slowly, in small bites. That's why this daily format is so perfect. I invite you to take a few minutes for yourself each day to step away from the material world and spend some time with your Self. Meditate on the meaning of Sanaya's message, and contemplate how you can apply it in your life. Used in this way, Sanaya's *Love Beyond Words* will do more than inspire you … it will transform your life.

January 1

LOVED BEYOND WORDS

You are loved beyond words. Do you yet realize this? The sun rises in your honor. The moon beams its smile upon you each night. The earth revolves around you. You are the center of the universe, the heart of the world. You are the love that you seek.

Seek not outside yourself for God's love. Roll in it now. Bathe in it. Bask in it, for it is all around you and within you. It is you. You need only open your eyes to this truth to transform your life.

Wipe away your sorrows in an instant with this knowingness of who and what you are. If you do not yet understand this truth, set it as your principal desire in life to know your Self as love. Pray fervently for this awakening, then open your eyes.

January 2

NOT OF THIS WORLD

"Be in the world, but not of it"—one of the wisest sayings you can follow. You walk for a time in a human's shoes, but you need not assume the clothing of the body as your identity. In fact, it is this very outer clothing that does mask the real you—one who is one with the Creator. Unmask yourself. Disrobe completely from the body and see that all are alike. There is no longer the competition of who wears the finest clothes, who owns the finest things, and who has the greatest beauty. There is only Love and the expression of Love toward others.

You need not die to learn this truth. You need not die to act as a loving spirit without a body. Be in the world, as you are now—with a body and all the trappings of life in the physical plane—but be of Spirit in mind and in loving action in each moment. There you will find peace—when all attachments are gone, when all fear has been replaced by the understanding that you are Spirit here and now.

Be in the world. Sit back. Observe and nod your head at all you see and say, "That's Life … good and bad … That's Life." You are merely here to play a part. How will you play it today?

January 3

BIRTHDAYS … EVERY DAY

It matters not how many birthdays you have. What matters is how you fill those days. Do you use your time in this body to love? Do you use this time to grow? If you see a new wrinkle, do you bemoan the fact that the body is changing, or do you celebrate how much you are learning?

The body is naught but a tool. Use it to indicate to you when you are out of alignment in your thoughts. It will clench, tighten, and sicken if your thoughts are not pure and loving. Relax. Thank the body for telling you so clearly that the spirit is being suppressed. Set your spirit free by releasing fear and worry, by releasing judgment and anger. First and foremost, do not judge the body, but thank it for its lessons—for being the perfect outward mirror of what is happening inside.

Celebrate your birthday each morning that you open your eyes. "Thank you, Spirit, for giving birth to this day, and for giving me the opportunity to learn and to love."

January 4

HARMONY

Fever means the head burns hot.
A healthy body have you not.
From where does come this bad dis-ease?
From trying hard ego to please.

When ego's role you focus on
You fail to see it's all a con—
A false belief that you reside
In a form you can divide.

You are not the form at all.
It's spirit's name who you does call.
"Acknowledge me," this voice does cry.
"My presence please do not deny."

There's only love, not separate lives.
In spite of how the ego strives
To make you think you stand apart
Instead of all joined by the heart.

When separation you believe,
The cells inside you do deceive.
And in this way you do create
A most unpleasant inner state.

The end result is often ills
That lead you to resort to pills
When illness could have been prevented
If from deception you repented.

See now your oneness with all things
And feel the peace that seeing brings.
Give love to self and to your brother
For, in fact, there is no other.

All are reflections of the Source.
Through all veins God's love does course.
So keep this always close at mind
And far more harmony you'll find.

January 5

NO EXPECTATIONS

Be patient with each other. Be mindful of the demands you do place on those besides yourself to conform to your desires. Why should you all be alike? Why should others think exactly as you do? This life is to be experienced in all of its many expressions.

All that you should hope for from another is that they extend love and kindness to you and others, just as you strive to do. But even over this you have no control. The only thing you control is your own thoughts and actions. Let your thoughts be compassionate and understanding when others do not meet your expectations. Let your actions be loving and helpful. If not, frustration and anger will be your experience. Be at peace within, no matter what transpires without. It is always up to you.

January 6

BE AWARE

Bad news always brings a reaction. For some it is weeping, for others gnashing of the teeth, and for yet others lashing out in anger. Do you realize that all of these are learned and programmed responses? The words you hear hold meaning to you based on thoughts held in your conscious and subconscious mind. Why is it that there can be such varied responses to the same news? Why is it that some, upon hearing what others consider bad news, can react with peaceful calm? It is because of their personal programming.

Do you realize that your reaction to all news, whether good or bad, is always a choice? The first response will always be an automatic reaction, but after that you are not a puppet on strings. Never forget that you arise from the Source of All Love. Your role always is to be as the Source and express your Self. If you can see through the shock of any instant and remember Who you are, your subsequent reactions can come from a much higher place. When you react with love instead of fear, you do help the cells of your body as well as raise all consciousness which surrounds you. Never forget who you are. In this there is true power.

Be aware.

January 7

SING!

Be not bashful. Sing the praises of Life at the top of your voice. What is singing, but the joyful expression of that which you feel in your heart. Music does indeed carry a vibration—each note resonating with various human emotions. Choose songs which uplift you, which make your heart soar, and sing with all of your might. It matters not if you can carry a tune, merely that you express the love inside through the voice.

Let there be a joyous noise as you rejoice in being alive. Why do you think one speaks of a "choir" of angels? Angels know naught but love and sing in perfect harmony. Sing loud and sing long. Sing with your radio, with your favorite singer, or all alone where no one can hear you. It matters not. Your spirit longs to be set free. Let it soar on the notes of your voice, and feel the freedom. Feel the love. That is the music of the Maker.

January 8

NOURISHMENT FOR THE SOUL

A baker's dozen refers to when one receives more than one has paid for. All of life can be a baker's dozen when the currency is love.

So many people give love expecting love in return. Be aware that there will always be misers in your pathway who hold onto their love with a tight fist. Let this matter not. Love them anyway. You will always receive more in return than you give. The problem comes when you fail to understand that all is One. So, if the love does not come back from an individual you have identified, do not be disappointed. It will come from another and more.

Be not demanding, but let your love flow freely. Let it fall where it might. Like the baker's dough, spread it out and watch it grow. As the baker, you create something from nothing: nourishment for the souls of others in the form of your love.

January 9

LABELS

Fathers look after their children with utmost care. Mothers cradle their children in their arms and provide comfort. The unconditional love of a parent goes beyond boundaries. It is for this reason that much of mankind does refer to the Great Source of All That Is as "Father" or "Father-Mother God." We wish you to know that you may put any label you like upon this Benevolent Source of All Love. Choose any title or label which to you references the extension of love, limitless creativity, and limitless awareness. Call this "Great Creator," "Great Artist" ... the list is endless, for all that is arises from one Source, one Divine Mind ... and all from the desire to experience and express beauty.

Your Source has no body, for that would imply limitation. You have been gifted with a body so that Your Source can experience and express love and beauty as you. So call this Source whatever loving term resonates with you, but in the end, when you have fully awakened, you will add one other term to your list that signifies all love and beauty and that unites you with your true Self: not "Father," not "Mother," but "I," for you ... are ... That.

January 10

PEACE IN THE DEPTHS

Allow yourself to sink deep. Feel as if falling slowly into a deep chasm. There at the bottom lies total stillness. Away from all distractions there is peace. Just as at the bottom of the ocean, it is still. The disturbances and waves on the surface may still be there far above, but when you settle below, you experience the calm. This is the state you are seeking in meditation. It is a state of unperturbed consciousness.

This deep calm lies within you at all times. When you experience it repeatedly by sitting in the silence, you come to know that this peace is not only a part of you, but it is your natural state. A simple visualization will help you to get there. Be as the pebble that causes ripples with your thoughts on the surface, then surrender and sink slowly to the peaceful bottom of the sea of consciousness. Allow your mind to settle there for a while on a regular basis, and far more peaceful will be your days.

January 11

TEACH YOUR CHILDREN WELL

You spend so much time educating children in practical matters, such as how to add two and two, and how to read *Dick and Jane.* Years and years they spend in formal schooling, yet who does guide them in this grand School of Life? It is true that all are on their own path, and beliefs will vary, but is it not true that there are certain truths which are the same for all? The greatest lesson lies in what you call the Golden Rule, found in nearly all of your organized religions in some form. Should this not be taught to your children each day until each member of mankind can never forget it?

Whether or not one can add numbers or read letters matters little at the end of this physical life. But whether one has learned The Prime Lesson makes a world of difference when one moves toward the Light and asks, "How did I spend my days? Did I treat each one as a brother or sister? Did I love them as I love myself?" The goal of life should be to answer this question with a resounding "Yes!"

Teach your children well, and as you do, make sure that as the teacher, you do practice what you teach.

January 12

IN AN AVALANCHE

There are times when all of your troubles seem to pile up at once. You wonder, is this an avalanche with everything falling upon you and seemingly suffocating you? There, in the center, is a little breathing space. It is completely quiet and dark at first, yet stay there but a few minutes looking with eyes closed, and you will see a tiny pin prick of light. This is your salvation. From this light comes a sense of peace … the knowingness that you are not alone and are well protected.

No matter what is going on around you, this quiet space with the breathing room and tiny light is your sacred place to which you can retreat at any time. Go there often and watch as that light grows until it not only fills you and surrounds you, but until you realize that it IS you. Then, my friend, it will not matter what befalls you. You will know that you can see your way through it in peace.

Peace be with you.

January 13

THE UNLIMITED SOURCE

Batteries ... they do take stored energy and convert it into something useful—usable energy which you can call on at any time to make your small appliances work. Your body is like a battery. It does store up energy which you then use to run the very parts of yourself. But like your small Duracells, do not the cells of your body run down and need replenishment?

Plug yourself into the Great Battery Charger on a regular basis. Receive a supply of revitalizing energy at any time—yes, by stopping the frenetic action to and fro and resting, of course. But from where comes the replenishing flow of energy which you do take on during rest? Ask yourself this question.

Your energy supply comes from the Unlimited Source. Should this Source wish for you to no longer continue your lessons in the great School of Physical Life, your physical battery would run down completely. But from moment to moment your Source replenishes the body and the spirit as well. Treat the body well, and give it time to recharge. And while you are resting or sitting in the silence, give thanks that you have an ever-present light inside you, fueled by the loving energy of your Source.

January 14

THE SUN ALWAYS RISES

You watch the sun rise above the horizon and you rejoice at the start of another day. What new opportunities will it bring? If you do not see this new beginning in such a light, then we ask you to shine a very bright light onto your thoughts. Perhaps you are going through a difficult time in your life, but has not the sun arisen again to bring light into your life? It is clouds across the mind that do block out this realization.

The Great Spirit gave birth to the sun to bring you light and the hope of rebirth, renewal, and growth. The Great Spirit created you to experience the light, and to shine your own light upon others. No matter what challenges you face, the sun will always rise to shine upon you, and the light is always there within you. It is only you who can clear away the clouds. No matter what challenges you face, this realization that the light lies there within you can banish the darkness in an instant.

Yes, the sunset does remind you of the cycles of life. Within the physical world there are beginnings and endings. Change is the signature of the Divine Mind at work. But knowing that the sunrise always follows the sunset and that the sun never actually goes away, you find hope. The darkness is not lasting. The light is still there. This too shall pass.

January 15

PART OF THE LESSONS

Tribes of nations go to war …
What for?
They fight and kill each other,
Forgetting that the other one's a brother.

It is the governments that rule
Who do forget this is a school
Where all the same things here do learn
Where all inside for love do yearn.

It's through illusion they forget.
They see not the truth inside, and yet
Here and there does lie a glimmer
Of the light that in all does shimmer.

Give up not hope that love will prevail.
There is a happy ending to this tale.
For one day will be lifted the veil of illusion
And gone forever will be man's confusion.

If only through what you now call death
When the body takes its final breath.
For now you see this as an end
But it's then to you great hope we send.

For then you'll see with brand new eyes.
It's then all men do realize
That all the fighting was a game of man
A tiny blink in the overall plan.

The wars and destruction are part of the lessons
That in your soul do leave deep impressions,
And teach to all the importance of Life
Instead of raising a gun or a knife.

January 16

ON AGING

Allow yourself to grow older. Yes, you have a choice—between resisting and allowing. Allow the aches and pains. Allow the need for testing—the tests that come to you from both your doctors and from your life lesson teachers. You are here to learn, and you cannot learn unless you grow. This you call aging.

It is those who resist this very natural process who age faster than others. Do you see the irony? Resistance causes blockage of the rejuvenating, healing, energizing Life Force. Allow this natural process of aging to occur, and instantly you do feel better inside, in the very part of you which never ages. Retreat to that part of you which is pure spirit. Watch the aging process with great interest as you allow it to occur. Send compassion to the body as it serves you. Send compassion to others who do not understand the truths of the Spirit.

When you see a new wrinkle or undergo other milestones in the process of living a physical life, step into awareness of yourself as spirit and allow. Now there's a new wrinkle, is it not?

January 17

TRANSMUTE AND TRANSFORM

Bury your thoughts, and you think you've done away with them. But where do they go when you push them down or away? Thoughts are pure energy, and energy cannot be destroyed—merely transformed. Those thoughts that you leave behind continue to fester in the subconscious mind and can be seen in your energy field by those who can perceive these subtle energies.

So how do you make sure that thoughts which no longer serve you no longer affect you? You transform them. You replace them with thoughts of a higher frequency so that those thoughts of a lower frequency are subsumed and transmuted into new beliefs of a finer vibration. This does not happen by itself. First, realize that you did create the lesser thoughts of your own mind by believing illusions thrust upon you by a world steeped in illusion. Anything less than love is a lie and serves you not.

Step into that place in which you know yourself as pure Love, and from this place of creation create love-filled thoughts in which any other thought cannot survive—forced out, changed, and transmuted by love. This is transformation.

January 18

AT YOUR OWN PACE

You can lead a horse to water,
But you cannot make it drink.
Another's thoughts and actions
Are more habitual than you think.

It's not your place to say
What others think and do.
So worry not when how they act
Does not agree with you.

Each one is on his own sure path.
Each grows at his own pace.
And with perfect timing
His own lessons will he face.

So worry not of others.
Try not to keep control.
It's only you who needs to grow
As you develop your own soul.

If this thought does bring you trouble,
If you think all others need grow, too,
Then you've lost focus of the lesson
That there's only One of you.

January 19

EFFORTLESS

Expending effort is wasted effort. You need not try to do anything. To do anything, you need merely have the intention, the desire, and the knowledge that you are connected at all times with an Intelligence far greater than your own. With this knowledge, how could you fail at "doing"?

You may not achieve exactly what you want if your intentions are not aligned with The Greater Good. Ego intentions are often quite different from Spirit intentions. Turn your desires over to the Divine Mind. "Thy will be done" is an excellent phrase for finding freedom.

You need not try or expend worry when you do anything from a place of knowing that all is in perfect order always. Yes, of course you will need to "do"—to take action—but without trying. Do you see the difference? When there is no struggle, then you have surrendered ego and are allowing. Allowing is the doorway to freedom.

January 20

OF LIKE MIND

Do not bemoan the state of your world, for in the negativity of this mindset you do prolong the negativity. See instead that there is still Love at the essence of all things. Be that Love. Model that Love. Extend that Love. That is your only true role here and now and forever after.

No matter what goes on around you or within the body-mind, see and be only love, elsewise you are merely caught up in the same illusion as others who still live in illusion. There is only One Mind. Be of like mind with your Source and project light into the darkness. As you do so, you illuminate those around you.

January 21

ONE MIND

Dusty pages of a book …
Take a look.
Ancient words so wise
They come as a surprise.

Who knows from whence they come?
It matters not when day is done,
But the wisdom they contain
From the pages … much to gain.

Akashic Records some do call
Where is encompassed truly all
The knowledge that has ever been
The knowledge contained there within.

Release the blocks that you have placed
The limits that you thought you faced,
And know that all you've sought to know
Is there just like a movie show.

The records of all that is and was
Are there awaiting … why? Because
There's one great Mind that does the thinking
It's ever-expanding, never shrinking.

And so this book, this show, this "thing"
That to you all-knowingness will bring
Is there for you to seek and find
When you do realize, there's but One Mind.

January 22

BLESSED ARE THE MEEK

"Blessed are the meek, for they shall inherit the earth." These "meek" beings walk upon the earth and appear as powerless to those who misunderstand what true power is. Meekness does not imply weakness. Meekness is merely the act of surrendering effort and resistance.

There is no need to exert effort or to resist what surrounds you once you realize that you are Spirit at your essence, and nothing else is real. With this realization, all need to struggle vanishes, and meekness becomes power. You inherit the beauty and the harmony of the earth, for in nature lies the essence of Spirit. There is no chaos on earth, save that which has been created by the non-meek. Blessed are you always, but claim your true inheritance now through surrender. Do so, and you will never have felt more powerful.

January 23

THE ONLY BATTLE THAT MATTERS

Respond to all problems with love. It is the only way to find true peace. Yes, you always have a choice. Revert to the lower vibrations and lash out in self-protection, but what does that do for you? It only builds a wall of separation around you. Watch your thoughts carefully. If you find yourself clenching a fist and walling off your heart, your thoughts are the cause of this—not the actions of another. Step back away from the role of a solitary soldier and watch the battle scene from afar. What point is there in this scene? Who will come out the winner? Neither, if both sides do not walk off arm in arm.

Respond only with love, your greatest weapon against darkness.

January 24

TWO SIDES TO EVERY COIN

Everybody has a story.
Yours is one of many.
You see only one side.
There's a tail on every penny.

Be not so quick to judge
When one does do you wrong.
For outwardly and inwardly
They may sing a different song.

What troubles you, you oft don't show,
And others hide as well
The turmoil that they feel inside—
Their own internal hell.

So rather than reacting
With anger when confronted,
Stop and think, "What is the cause
For which I've been affronted?"

And though this cause may never show
Your waiting is a gift.
For in this pause you give the time
For love the soul to lift.

See not each one with judging eyes,
But feel within your heart.
You need not know another's tale
To play a healing part.

January 25

THE SCHOOL OF LIFE

You want to be an A student in the School of Life? Love with all your heart and soul. Yes, love your brother as yourself. Go out of your way to extend kindness, compassion, and love to all others. It matters not how much money you earn, how many books you write, beautiful sculptures you create, businesses you start. If these endeavors help to serve others, then this is "extra credit," but always what is in the heart is what matters most. You need not carry a heavy load of books nor study hard. Simply be who you are: pure Love at your essence, here to extend and express that love in all ways … always.

There are those who will fail in their lessons repeatedly. All are given remedial help. Tutors stand at your side ready to assist. Teachers are everywhere, providing you opportunities to raise your grade, but it is not a competition. There is truly only One of you in this school—one Heart, one Mind … all merely facets of the same jewel. Shine as brightly as you can in every moment to earn the gold star … the realization of who and what you are.

January 26

UNCONDITIONAL LOVE

The love of an animal is not to be denied. These are God's gift to man, most especially the domesticated animals you keep at your side as loving companions. These animals know nothing of past or future, of worry over things that have long gone and things that may never come to pass. They concern themselves only with the present moment and with their current needs. These needs are the same as yours: food, comfort, and shelter, to be sure, but also affection and relationship. They know nothing of withholding love, only of giving.

Humans should study these behaviors closely and model them if they wish to find peace and fulfillment. The unconditional love of a pet knows no bounds. They know not judgment. Their needs are quite simple, as are yours when you remove the leash of living as a human-being, which you yourself have placed around your neck, and live as the spirit-being that you are.

January 27

THE BEST ADDICTION

Do not rehash old memories. You hold onto them as if they were lifelines. Do you not realize that thoughts create emotions, and emotions create chemical changes within the body? The more you focus on a negative memory, the more of these chemicals course through your blood, to the point where the body craves this feeling which you have created. This creates a harmful cycle which perpetuates imbalance and disharmony, leading to dis-ease.

When the habitual images and thoughts of a traumatic event come to mind, be aware of them. At that instant it is most important to realize that staying with this image and wallowing in the subsequent emotional-chemical reaction is a choice. The better choice is to gently nudge it outward, not downward. Send it toward the light and fill the remaining space with light. Flood your mind with love, and choose an alternate loving memory to take its place. Soon the body will no longer need this "fix" from the traumatic event and will ask instead for a love-fix. You control both. It is always a choice at the conscious level what you do with that which bubbles up from the subconscious level. Be addicted to love.

January 28

THE KEY TO MEDITATION

Sitting in the silence is not simply to enjoy a lack of noise. It is a time of communion with your Self. Understand well that your Self consists of the entire spectrum of Consciousness—the intricately linked minds of you, your guides, the great masters, and the Master of All That Is. You sit in the silence to know your connection with the All—to know yourself as pure consciousness and Love. If you merely sit in a chair to be quiet, then you will find rest, but this is stopping short of the true gift of meditation.

Whilst sitting in your chair, first give thanks, and know that your gratitude is well received. By whom? By all those who are there helping you through each moment. And now that you have consciously made this connection and are no longer under the false illusion that you are sitting in a chair alone, ask a question. It matters not the subject. It matters not whether big or little, heavy or trivial, spiritual or mundane … Ask a question knowing that it is being heard by Higher Intelligence, then let go of the need to hear an answer. Ask a question every time you sit in meditation. Soon you will see that your questions are being answered as the answers come in what to you are miraculous ways, but are, in fact, merely indicators that—lo and behold—you never were sitting in that chair alone.

Make this question-asking your daily habit and enter into a companionship with Spirit that is guaranteed to transform your life. Such an adventure that awaits you, Beloved, when you trust.

January 29

JITTERS

When the world seems to be moving faster than you are, begin with deep breathing. Slow down your racing thoughts just enough that the whisper of the Voice of Spirit can get through. "Relax," it says. There is never any need for worry when you turn over all results to the Universe and pray, "Thy will be done." It is only when you do forget that all is in perfect order always, and you forget that you are being guided always, that you do feel the jitters.

Jitter not. Use these quaking feelings as an indicator that you have temporarily forgotten who you are and are letting the ego side of yourself run the show. Bring Spirit to the forefront and feel the peace that quells the quaking body. You are never in charge anyway. It is only the ego's false belief that causes the disturbance. Surrender to the flow and step into the peaceful river of Life.

January 30

THE ART OF GIVING

Spare nothing when you give of yourself. Stinginess brings you nothing but emptiness. If you wish to experience the fullness of love, open your heart and give. Give of your heart with your voice, with your hands, with your time, and with your money. All of these were given to you not to hoard, but to hand over. Why? Because in giving, you connect with another soul and say, "What I have is yours. There is no difference nor distance between us. I recognize your value and wish you to recognize it as well."

Be a giving machine. Is not the body a most perfect machine? Yes, of course, it has breakdowns from time to time, but at its essence it is perfection—the perfect machine with which you can express the essence of the spirit which enlivens that machine. How better to express that essence than in giving to others what you truly are. The need to hold back merely serves as an indicator that you have not yet fully learned this Truth. Give yourself the gift of awakening.

January 31

TEAMWORK

The whole world revolves around one Truth: There is only one Mind running the show. Whose dream is it, anyway?

Is your life your own? You take far too much credit for your thoughts. You are part of a team of minds, all learning from each other ... some far more experienced than you on their different plane of existence. What is a team, but a group of individuals that works as one, all with the same purpose. You may feel as an individual player, but it is the team that matters most. What affects one, affects all. Renegades are detrimental to the group effort. Cohesiveness is the goal.

What is the purpose of your team? To spread love and light to the world. Do not go running off by yourself, but listen to the guidance of the Coach. At your level there are most certainly winners and losers. In the end, when all teams merge and competition ceases, then all will be winners. In the meantime, get with the Team.

February 1

UNSEEN HELPERS

A gathering of angels at your side …
It makes no sense to run and hide.
They come to teach and show the way—
A touch of grace that starts your day.

You always have this team of helpers with you. Can you imagine navigating this world completely alone? A frightening thought, perhaps, to those who do not realize how very much help surrounds them at all times. You are not a solo wanderer. You are part of All That Is—born of the Source of All Love. It is that same Love that wishes you to succeed in this experience you are having as you.

Success in spiritual terms is quite different than the material. May you have whatever material success you think you desire, but may your growth as a spirit-being be ever upward as you learn to see and be only love. This is when your team of unseen helpers is most present—when you place your focus on true success and ask for their help. Why, you will almost hear them singing, such is the joy engendered when you realize why you exist.

February 2

LET YOUR LOVE POUR

Feel your heart beat ...
At times it does pound.
A reminder that there
Is love all around.

The heart is the center
Of the emotional field
Wherein your true essence
As love is revealed.

Place your focus right there.
Bring it oft to the fore.
Then send out what you feel
And to this world you'll bring more.

To be loved is a blessing.
To give love, greater yet.
Go forth as a light –
And others' appetites whet.

Be so loving and kind
That when they see you they sigh,
For your love will be felt
Such that none can deny.

To feel love is a gift;
To spread it out even more.
So open your heart
And let your love pour.

February 3

FIND THE JOY INSIDE

Greet each day with joy, even when you find it hard to smile. Joy comes from within, not from what is happening around you. If you find yourself out of sorts, you are identifying with the external world. That which you perceive through the bodily senses is impermanent and leads to misperception.

When in need of a lift, when you forget what joy feels like, it is vitally important that you sit quietly, close out the outer world, and ask to experience your True Self. As you become practiced in doing this, it will become impossible not to raise your spirits as you raise your conscious awareness that you are spirit, not body.

Nothing outside of you matters. Nothing drags down the spirit. You, as Spirit, are pure joy and love. If you speak of feeling low or irritable, sad or angry, this is not of your spirit, but the body-mind. Again we say, sit and pray, and to you will return that well-spring of joy and peace, bubbling up from within to remind you that only Love is real.

February 4

BORROWED TIME

You speak of "borrowed time." What does this mean? It shows a belief that time is limited—that there is not enough of it to fulfill your desires in your time remaining here on earth. First you must understand that time is a construct of the human mind. Time has beginnings and endings and limitations. You as pure spirit have none of these. You as a human being in a body perceive that you have them all: beginning, end, and limitations. You cling so tightly to these beliefs, and then you fear when these endings and limitations come to pass.

Step back and see the greater picture with the eyes of the soul. This lifetime you are now experiencing is one of a continuous expression of You as Consciousness and Love. It is a great expression of creation … a great adventure. Far more Adventures in Consciousness await you. The only thing you have borrowed is a bit of dust and matter from your Mother Earth. Upon its return to dust, the Real You will continue on living and learning. Have no fear.

February 5

GIVE NO POWER TO ILLUSION

There is no such thing as a devil, if by this word you understand an actual entity who stands opposite of God. To understand this, you must first change your concept of God from an actual benevolent being to an intangible, yet fully benevolent and loving, conscious Force which is the source of all that is. If All That Is is loving and benevolent and all-powerful, then how, you may ask, can evil exist?

Evil is the result of the false illusion of the ego of man—that part of the human consciousness that does falsely believe it is separate from God. Off marches the ego, making decisions as an individual out of alignment with Love. The results at times are so far misaligned with Love that you do call this "evil." Such acts are not perpetrated by an entity with horns and a pitchfork. This image is symbolic. As a metaphor for evil, the devil exists in the ego of each human. It is the choice and the main task of each human being to realize the truth—that separation from God never happened. All else is illusion. When will you stop dreaming?

February 6

INTENTION

Deliberate intention produces results far beyond mere meandering of the mind. The human being so often wonders why he or she fails to see in this life that which they desire. Desire is but one part of the crucial equation of creation. Intention is the key. First arises the desire for a particular outcome, then it is up to you to focus your consciousness in such a way that you see no other outcome. This is intention.

Understand that you are but a focus of Pure Consciousness. As such, the desire and intention of the Creator will always hold more sway in outcomes over your personal desires. Do not struggle, but pray that your intentions be in alignment with that of your Source. This is when the act of surrendering to the Greater Good becomes an act of great power.

Make it your greatest desire and your greatest intention to serve your fellow human being, and all worldly desires will lose their luster as you come into alignment with your true purpose on earth.

February 7

ALWAYS GUIDED

You stand on the edge of a cliff—the bottom far below. Such a decision you face: "Should I take this leap? A jump such as this will change my life." At times your decisions are like this … monumental, with great consequences. How to know whether or not to take the leap or make no move at all? Have we not told you, we will catch you if you fall? Always are you guided, yet you are so often undecided. It's merely a matter of having trust, and for this reason, surrender is a must.

Surrender to the will of God. Such submission you may find odd, but never will we let you fail. Most certainly, outcomes may differ from what you expected. Be that as it may, you will realize growth. There are lessons to be learned from every decision and every action. The lessons, we assure you, are always far more gentle when your decisions are guided from within.

February 8

SEE WITH NEW EYES

A blind man sees the world quite differently than those with physical sight. He forms his impressions by attuning more greatly to his other physical senses. In this way, his perceptions are what you might consider impaired. But why are his perceptions any less valid than one who uses yet other forms of sensing with the body alone?

We wish you to know that any human being who forms his perceptions based solely on input from the physical senses is a blind man. The body is a useful tool for operating in the physical world, but that world is only a temporary existence. You exist in another world side by side, here and now, yet you are blind to this higher existence if your sole focus is on the physical. Shift your focus, my friend. Walk each moment with soul focus, and expand your perceptions infinitely.

See Reality with the eyes of the soul—with the heart—and all wisdom, power, and love will be yours. These attributes lie within you now, for they are the attributes of your Source, but dimmed they are until you shine the light inward instead of focusing only outward. Be not blind to Reality. See with the soul and your path will be clear.

February 9

WHO LOVES YOU?

You have a pledge you learned as a child: "One nation, under God, indivisible ..." You, my child, are like this nation—one being, under God, indivisible. You are the ocean and the wave. You are the sun and the sunbeam. You are the forest and the tree, the tree and the twig. It is true, the twig would die if separated from the tree. The tree, standing alone, loses its identity with the forest. The sunbeam and the wave are yet closer to their source, for it is impossible to separate the two from their source.

Are you beginning to understand your relationship with your Source? You try to stand alone—to believe yourself independent, but you can only stand alone for but a short while. What is the Source of the water you drink, the food you require, and the air you breathe? What is the Source of your companionship? What is the Source of your very thoughts?

You cannot live without breathing, yet we ask you ... who breathes you? And when you cease breathing and find that you still exist, it is that very thought –the realization that you exist—that is of your Source as well. The Creator thinks through you, breathes through you, loves through you. Who loves you? Your indivisible God.

February 10

EGO'S LAST GASP

"I can do this myself!" you do claim. It is this need to be independent that does keep you from experiencing true Love. Why do you need to be the one with all the answers, the one to always be right, the one to have your way? Such rebellion! Do you see how it keeps you separate?

Look upon all others not as competitors, but as equal cells in the body of God. Do the cells of your own body fight each other? Yes, at times they do, and this you call "dis-ease." Cease the need to be first, to be right, and to have your own way. Allow your fellow cells to contribute to your harmony and health by surrendering this thing you call the "will," and you will experience far greater peace.

Recognize the urge to control outcomes as the ego's strangled cry for attention. Pay him no heed. The voice of Love is far more subtle, far less insistent, for Love knows that sooner or later you will come around and pay attention. Why wait? Thank the ego now for its many years of service and give your full attention to the Voice of Love.

February 11

THE ART OF CREATION

Start at what you call the beginning—your so-called "Big Bang." This was only the bringing into existence of yet another reality in which God could experiment and play with creation. You do this every moment of your life, for have we not told you repeatedly that you are the Creator in form? A facet, of course, but still quite capable of taking the tiniest of ideas and turning them into actuality. All that exists, including you, began as a thought, which increased in vibration to become desire, followed by intent, and the result became something to be experienced.

Look around you. You and those around you have created all that you now experience. If you do not wish to continue this particular experience, begin with that idea and create the surroundings and experiences of your heart's desire. It is only your ignorance of your great creative abilities which does keep you locked in one experience. All is by choice. Create anew if you are unhappy. Begin first, however, by creating the thought in your mind that all is Love. This will awaken all other possibilities as you bring your Self slowly out of your slumber.

February 12

THROW DOWN YOUR SWORD

Throughout your life you will face a variety of tests. There are few tests greater than to love those who hurt you. You will face the deaths of loved ones, and you will face illness. These do require understanding of the nature of Reality, but the greatest understanding comes when you can look upon one who acts out of fear and ignorance and send that one love.

So many in your world do not know who they are. They are blind to their self as Spirit. Because of this, they do hurtful things. Their words and actions are dark, and can be painful if perceived as something that can hurt you. Understand well that nothing can hurt You-as-Spirit. It is only the ego that feels pain. The soul is pure Love.

When pained by another, this is a duel between egos. Throw down your sword and surrender the ego. This is an act of power … an act of awakening. The other may continue to spar, but without an adversary, he will have to look elsewhere. By modeling right action yourself, perhaps your brother may actually catch a glimpse in your mirror of his true nature. And perhaps not, if that is his choice. Struggle not with another's darkness. Worry only if your own light burns brightly enough.

February 13

THE ONLY RULE YOU NEED

So many rules you do place upon yourselves ... morals, dictated by others. "Thou shalt do this and that, but never that or this" ... rules to live by, based on judgments. There is but one rule, one law, which you can follow and with which you can never go wrong, and that is the Law of Love.

"Love thy brother as thyself, and love thy God with all thy heart." All else—all other rules—follow this one rule. "Is it wrong to do this or that?" you may wonder, and the answer lies in this statement. It is the Golden Rule. Are you hurting another by your actions? You always know the answer if you look within your heart. This is conscience.

True, some of your fellow human beings have buried their conscience so deeply within layers of ego that they do need the rules of man, but you who remain conscious that you are created in the image of the Father, need only this one rule. Begin by loving yourself, then it becomes far easier to love your brother as yourself. Seek the Father within to know what real Love is.

February 14

FOCUS

Sing a song of happiness
For all is quite in order.
There will be no lack or pain
When you go across the Border.

Heaven's what you call this place
Where naught but beauty does abound.
But what you fail to see is all
The beauty now around.

You tend to focus on the things
That trouble you the most
Instead of giving focus
To your great and mighty Host.

The things of God are perfect;
The things of man not quite.
To know perfection is your task—
To see the world with brand new sight.

What's Real is what's eternal.
Your spirit is like that.
So put your fears and doubts aside
And know that Heaven's where you're at.

February 15

ON COMPROMISE

Compromise, my friend. You are in this world to share… to share the experience of Life. You are one focus of the Consciousness that you call "God." All else that you see—all living things—are also focuses of the One Source. Were you here alone, there would not be the richness of experience nor the great variety of lessons to learn. And so, as others fulfill their dreams and wishes, you are given a choice to enjoy their dreams with them or to enjoy your own. Always it is a choice.

Not always do the dreams coincide. When this happens, you have the opportunity to give up one dream or the other, or to enjoy both to a lesser degree. Much more is to be gained by enjoying both through the act of compromising, for as we have already stated, you do learn far more through relationships with others than by spending all of your time alone. Work out a compromise and reap the benefits of combining alternate facets of the God Force. Such richness is available to you if you only step outside your self-imposed boundaries.

February 16

IT'S VERY SIMPLE

The farther afield you go in your explorations, the more confused you do become. "Are there aliens? What is this 'ascension' for which some are preparing? Are there portals through which mere mortals can pass?" Do not concern yourself with finding such answers. There are infinite paths down which you may wander … many branching off to the sides and taking you away from your main journey. The goal is always to come closer to your understanding of Reality.

The Reality of which we speak is quite simple and quite basic: You are one with the Divine Mind. You are a spirit-being here and now. There is naught but Love. And that is it. All else is superfluous chatter which takes your focus away from the One True Voice.

You need do nothing nor learn anything else but this most basic of messages, which can be narrowed down to one simple word: Love. It is both a thing and an action—a noun and a verb—but again, it boils down to one simple word … the essence of all things … and you are It.

February 17

WHERE TO PLACE YOUR ATTENTION

Little children know nothing of fear. They learn this. When new to this world, you were as pure as the Spirit which animates you. Your needs were met, and you were content—until you looked outside yourself and saw the world. The world showed you needs you knew nothing of, but once seen, they became desires. Desires unfilled became dissatisfaction and fear of not having them fulfilled. Your focus shifted entirely from the peace and joy of simply "being" to an external focus where peace and joy come and go, intermingled with unmet desires of things you have falsely come to believe that you need for your satisfaction.

Do you see how nothing outside of yourself can ever bring you the full peace, joy, and satisfaction that you came into the world knowing fully?

Why does the world love little children? There you see the reflection of the Spirit inside you … pure joy, pure innocence, pure love, pure "being." This state rests inside you now, only waiting to be remembered. Seek not outside yourself for ephemeral pleasures. All things and all physical beings outside of your Self will come and go. The true Self is eternal. All Spirit-Selves are linked for eternity. Place your focus there—on the spirit-self of yourself and others. There lies the peace and joy that all men seek.

February 18

HERE, NOW, AND FOREVERMORE

The loss of a loved one is one of the greatest trials you face in this physical world. We do stress the latter, for in the spirit world we know not of loss. Spirit is eternal. Consciousness expressing itself as you for a while in a physical body has a beginning and an end, for matter comes and goes, but that loving Consciousness goes nowhere. It exists here, now, and forevermore, everywhere.

If you truly realized this in your heart and mind, you would look upon a lifeless body and thank it for its service to your loved one, knowing full well that you are not talking to your loved one, but the vessel that they used for a while. And then, having thanked the body, you would step back, close your eyes, and talk to your loved one, who continues on here, now, and forevermore, everywhere.

Though you may not see them and can no longer touch a vessel which never was the true loved one, know that the true loved one hears you clearly. They need not ears, for they are now as they have always been and as you are, Beloved, pure spirit, pure consciousness … the same loving being you know in your heart, listening to your thoughts and sending back to you thoughts of love until you meet again.

February 19

KING OF ALL YOU SURVEY

Today we create a story for you…

Once upon a time, there lived a great king. He sat in his castle atop a hill. All thought that for his power and might he had all that he did need. They envied him his treasures and the glory—the adulation of the people he ruled. Were they to look inside the heart of the king, they would have found there an emptiness that none of the king's riches could fill.

This is a simple story, and you understand the analogy. Rest not your focus on external things. Envy not those in power, nor those with riches, for is it not true that the greatest of riches comes from a full and loving heart? Are not the happiest people on your earth those who have discovered this truth? You are the king of all you survey. Use your power to rule with love, and all the world is yours.

February 20

YOU ARE SPECIAL

Humility is a virtue. Treasure it. There is nothing to be gained by thinking you are more special than any other. You are unique, indeed, for all are endowed with unique abilities and talents, but all are equally special. Judge not another based upon appearances, actions, or lack of actions. Judge only yourself. Are you expressing your true nature at every opportunity?

Careful now. What is your true nature? It is that part of you that is truly special. It is that part of every human being that is truly special. It is the spirit. The spirit is Love. To express your special-ness, be loving. Speak only loving words. Have only loving thoughts. Take only loving actions. Now wouldn't that be special? Wouldn't that be unique? You wish to feel special … to be thought of as special? Be your Self.

February 21

LOCK AWAY YOUR TROUBLES

Confine your troubles to a box. Put them there for safekeeping. Put a lock on the box and peer inside from time to time when you need a reminder of why you came to this life on earth. Place a label on the box: "My Life Lessons," then sit back and stare at the box. Ponder its contents from afar. How have you chosen to deal with them? How have you allowed them to change the course of your life, to affect your emotions, your health, and your relationships? Sitting back like this, pondering your box of troubles from afar, you are safe. They are safely tucked away and cannot affect you. In this state you can be peaceful, allowing your troubles to simply sit there locked away, harmless and neutral.

Now, will you open that box again? Of course you will. Your life lessons are in there. But know that at any time you are completely free to shut the lid again, click the lock, sit back, and observe that harmless box from that place of peace that is always there for you to sit in. Go there often—at will—and you will be far more peaceful for it.

February 22

CONSCIOUS TRANSMISSIONS

The human body serves as an antenna for the waves of energy and information in which you at all times are swimming. This is why you do best to keep the spine straight while in meditation. But understand that you are not just a receiver of energetic information, but a transmitter as well. Every thought you think goes out from you, radiating into the universe and having an effect on all that your thought-wave touches. Think how you can affect your world by consciously creating your thoughts and deliberately focusing them when you wish to see a desired result.

Be a conscious creator, not an unfocused transceiver. If you are not happy with the circumstances in your life, this is an indicator that your thoughts are out of alignment with your desires. Stand tall, ask for and receive guidance through your internal antenna, then send out to the universe thoughts and visions of that which you wish to see in your life. It is not magic. Things do not happen by themselves. You are a co-creator of the universe. Do so responsibly and always with love.

February 23

THE GREATEST LESSON YOU CAN LEARN

You never stop learning. The doors of the School of Life are always open. So many lessons are you sent, but the curriculum is always the same. The subject is how to be the loving soul that you are at all times. Think of every situation in which you could possibly find yourself. If you were to choose a loving response to each one, your soul would grow. Those around you may not reap the benefits of your love if they are too closed off to the knowledge of who and what they are, but you would most certainly advance in your own soul's evolution, which is why you exist in the first place.

You are God expressing Itself. Put another way, you are Love expressing Itself. Each time you fail to do this, you make no progress and find no peace, for only when you align your self with your Self do you finally feel at home … at One. It is quite easy to do, yet so many of you make it harder than you must. Love. Simply love and be Love—not to gain anything from others, but to gain the World inside yourself. This is the greatest lesson you can learn.

February 24

GET ON WITH IT

Memories of bygone days ... you focus on these, remembering better times ... happier times when you were younger in years, more youthful in your thoughts, with a body that moved more gracefully. What is the matter with now? Nothing at all. You have created this "now." It is all part of the great adventure of your life. You are playing a role for now. In this role you inhabit a body that ages. It has no choice but to do so. But within that body, you are pure consciousness, creating new experiences in every moment. Are they worse than those you had in the past or better? What difference? All you have is this very moment. What will you do with it? That, my friend, is what makes this an adventure—not what you did in the past, not what you will do at some unforeseen time, but how you live right here and now, for here you are, and isn't that grand?

You exist. You are. You think. You create, and you go on creating. So go on. Get on with it. What will you create today? Love and peace? Jolly good. Then, you are beginning to understand.

February 25

WHY YOU ARE HERE

In a world of pain and suffering,
You might ask, "Why am I here?"
The answer is quite basic:
To be that which you hold most dear.

What is it that you treasure?
What brings your greatest joy?
The Force that dwells inside you …
The greatest tool you can employ.

It's love that lives there in you.
It's love that all do seek.
So why is it of emptiness
That so many often speak?

They suffer for they fail to see
They are the source of what they lack.
And with this misperception
Their fellow man they do attack.

Your purpose, then, is simple—
To uncover all the lies …
To bring forth what lies hidden
And expose it to the skies.

Be the shining light you are—
A beacon that pours forth
The love that's always been there
Like a compass pointing north.

Shine brightly, do not seek the light,
For love and light is what you are.
You need not look outside yourself;
You are the Great North Star.

February 26

YOU HAVE TO WORK AT IT

You hear the sounds of trucks on the road. This is the sound of busy people doing their work so early in the morning. You need these workers with their discipline to keep your society operating. Do you not realize that you require the same discipline to maintain your awareness of yourself as Spirit? This is part of the dream of life in which you are immersed—the constant falling back into the illusion that what you see is reality. The dream will always try to pull you in, and the ego loves this, for only when you buy into the illusion of separation does the ego thrive.

Work hard to remember the truths of the spirit. Find a mantra each day that you can repeat to yourself as you walk about and drive your trucks and do your work. In this way, as you repeat your "phrase of the day" you can be in the world but not of it. "What kind of phrase?" you ask. Any words or sentences that remind you that you are Spirit, that you exist only to express your spirit-nature as pure love, and that love is all there is. What more do you need?

February 27

IN THE EYE OF THE STORM

Peace is a gift—a glittering treasure like a golden coin you find buried in the sand. You pick it up and think, "Oh, look what I have found! I am so lucky!" But this gift of peace lies hidden within you always. It is part of the game of life that you do search for it and find it. The grains of sand of your life blow back and forth, oft times burying your peace in giant drifts, but always it lies waiting to be uncovered. You find it, then the wind blows again and covers it up.

When will you learn to not let the winds affect you? This is a learned skill, and again, it is the reason you have come here: to learn not to be buffeted by every breeze, but to stand firmly and hold onto your treasure—your inner peace … to stand in the calm eye in any storm, looking outward and knowing that you are not part of the storm, but merely an observer of it.

Funny thing about peace … the more of it you experience, the stronger it grows as you come to realize that no storm, no wind, can truly hurt you, for you are the peace you seek.

February 28

A NEW OPENING WINDOW

What is time, but a construct of your environment to aid you in identifying experiences in a linear fashion. You can look upon experiences which you have already had and call that your past. You can imagine experiences yet to come and call that your future, but all you truly have is this moment here and now. How will you use it?

Yes, this a theme to which we return quite often, but the whole point of your existence is to learn to use the moment now to express your Divinity. For this reason, what you did in the past matters not. What you think of doing in the future matters not. All that matters is, are you thinking loving thoughts right now? The next time you open your mouth, in that now-moment, will you produce loving words? If not, then you have missed an opportunity, but because you always find yourself in a new now-moment, you are free to try again. The more you succeed in thinking, speaking, and being only Love, the greater is this experience you call Life, and the more Love flows into it. What is "now"? A **N**ew **O**pening **W**indow to let in and out more love and light into your world.

March 1

MIND YOUR THOUGHTS

Hansel and Gretel—two fairy-tale figures who lived in the woods. Brother and sister in a gingerbread house. Is this fantasy? No more fantasy than buying into the illusion that you are powerless to create your environment. If you wished to live in a house of gingerbread, you could do so, such is your creative power. "But it would not last!" you cry. And this is so, were you to cease creating, but understand that creation never ceases—ever. Should the rains come, you would erect a tarp or barrier atop your special house. Should animals come to feed on the walls, you would build a fence, or better yet, disassemble the house and let the animals feed.

"Such a silly story today," you say, but is it? Is not your life one constant act of creation? You have a thought … a crazy idea. You turn this thought into an image in your mind, and then you do go forth and create a physical manifestation of this thought-image. Do you not see that all that surrounds you, including your very body, did arise from the very same process? You are as your Creator. What will you create today? Mind your thoughts carefully, for they have more power than most of your brothers and sisters are aware.

March 2

A TWINKLING STAR

Comes the dawn ...
And with it new surprises.
What will happen today
As the sun rises?

You know not the answer
For yours is to wait
And watch it unfold
As you discover your fate.

But are you a puppet
Whose arms move on strings?
Acting only when forced,
Knowing not what life brings?

Or do you create
What unfolds in each hour?
Have you any idea
Just how vast is your power?

Each cell in your body
Is aware of its role.
All work thus together
To enliven the whole.

But just as your cells
And your organs – your heart
Make up the whole body,
You, too, are a part.

Each system, each human
Is part of something quite large.
Each one individual
Of his Self is in charge.

But working together
You form something much greater.
A cell in the body
Of the One Great Creator.

So while independent
Your actions may seem,
Your role is quite vital
In the Big Cosmic Dream.

Take each action with care
For important you are.
In the vast sky of creation
You're one twinkling star.

March 3

CYCLES

Night turns into day, and day into night. The cycles of life are everywhere. You have your four seasons, your tides, your monthly changes, your birth and death. Yes, this too, is a cycle. Have you found anything in life which does not experience rebirth … recycling? Even your scientists know that energy is recycled, and have we not told you that you are pure energy … pure consciousness? Then why would you not experience recycling as well?

The part of you that you know as "you" will always be accessible, for energy cannot be destroyed, merely transformed. And so, while your physical body may be recycled into dust to form some other form someday, your consciousness as well will be recycled. But those who know you will always recognize that aspect of you when you meet again on the other side. Fear not that your loved ones will not be waiting for you when you have passed through this current cycle you call life. Those aspects of the Great Soul you come to know and love will be there and are there now.

But where is "there"? It is here, now, as all energy cycles around you. You merely need attune to the vibration, which cycles, does it not? How do your scientists measure energy? As a frequency. And how do they measure frequency? In cycles. All of life consists of energy and cycles, and you are That.

THE FOCUS OF LOVE

The heart is the focus of love. The heart in the physical body is naught but a mechanical pump, but without this pump, the vital nutrients and oxygen which the physical body requires would not circulate via the bloodstream and feed the hungry body. You could not exist without this organ.

On a spiritual level, you could not exist without the heart as the seat of love. This energy center gathers and circulates the energy of love. Love is the highest vibration, and were it not for the heart center, which collects and sends outward the vibration of love, all would wither and cease to exist, for love truly does make the world go 'round.

There is naught but Love. You have heard it said that God is Love, and this is true, for there is naught but God. God is all that is. All that you see is a manifestation of God-Love. Focus today on the heart. Pump love freely into your world and throughout your body, and see if you don't create beauty in this way.

March 5

GIVE CREDIT WHERE CREDIT IS DUE

Remove "mine" and "yours," and what is left, but One. All is One, but it is the fact that you perceive differentiation when you look about you that causes misunderstanding. Does one finger of the hand say, "That finger is yours, and this finger is mine."? Are not all fingers joined? Are they not all part of the same hand? Do they not function individually, but serve the greater good? What good does it do to say "mine" and "yours" when there is only one hand?

Focus not on your self today, but on the Self, and know that all that you see is of It. There is the appearance and the mass consciousness acceptance of "mine," but all is merely borrowed from the Source. Give credit where credit is due, and serve your purpose well. It is fine to be Self-ish, when you finally realize what the true Self is and serve it well.

March 6

IMAGINE INTO REALITY

What is imagination, but the creative use of the mind. What is the world in which you exist, but the creative use of the Mind of God—of Spirit. You were born of the imagination of the Divine Mind—a thought which became an image, which took form, and then became matter. You are not separate from God. You are part of that Divine Mind. As such, you are divine.

Use your divinity to create beauty and love. Use your divine imagination to give image to your thoughts. Imagine into reality that which you wish to see and achieve, and if you need help, call upon your guides, your angels, and your Highest Self ... God. The voice you hear in response may sound like your own, but listen closely. You may think, "This is only my imagination!" But how else could your guides, your angels, and your God speak to you?

March 7

PERCEPTION AND REALITY

There are vibrations all around you. Many of them you perceive through the physical senses, but many go unperceived. Think of one whose senses are a bit dulled. He hears not a certain pitch, and for him, this sound does not exist. It is not part of his reality, but to others it is quite evident. There are those in your world whose sensory perceptions are more heightened than others. "Is there truly a spirit world?" they are asked. "Do you really believe this?" And the question comes as a surprise. "You may not see or hear what I do," says the one whose instrument is more finely tuned, "but they are there. Trust me."

Trust us when we tell you that the spirit world is quite real. What is reality, but your current focus of consciousness and perception. Reality exists on many levels, in different dimensions, for consciousness is unlimited. You are experiencing one aspect of Reality now, but by expanding your consciousness through intention, you begin to perceive how truly unlimited you are.

How far can you expand your perception? Learning to do so is part of the great adventure you call Life.

A PERFECT FIT

Zippers … two sides of hard metal with teeth, that when joined together bring closure and firmly hold two pieces of cloth as one. The teeth fit together as a puzzle, perfectly joined one after another, yet if not aligned properly at the start, there is no closure; there is malfunction.

You have two sides to your being: an ego side, which is quite necessary to operate in the physical world, and a spirit side, which is your eternal self—that which you have come here to uncover and express. It is quite possible for the two sides of yourself to fit together beautifully whilst in this physical experience. It is simply a matter of finding the proper alignment.

When your life seems out of sorts, there is a gap between the two sides—the zipper cannot knit together. Seek the proper balance between operating from the ego, which is useful when performing certain tasks, and from the Spirit-self, which knows no separation, only love. When you have found the balance, the zipper slides freely, the cogs fit together quite well, and you experience harmony.

Do not mistake the message—the spirit is your true Self. It is not a 50-50 proposition between spirit and ego. We merely wish you to acknowledge and honor the two sides of yourself you now experience and seek balance between the two—a perfect fit.

March 9

FAN THE FLAMES

A light you shine
With a fire so bright
That all can feel it
Even had they no sight.

This is what happens
When God's love you know.
And through your actions
His Light you do show.

Hide not this Light,
But let it shine
And all will then sense
That this Light is Divine.

All have this Light,
But in some it is dim.
They first need to discover
That Light there within.

It burns there just waiting
To be thus discovered.
For a light such as this
Shall not remain covered.

What to do if your light
Feels like only an ember?
Simply love all you can
And then you'll remember

That this Light's who you are.
It has always been you.
When love you do show
You'll discover it's true.

Love all who you see.
Hold them all in your heart,
Then this ember inside
Will awake with a start.

Any longing you had
Will no longer remain.
When with love you do act
You do fan your own flame.

March 10

WHO'S IN CHARGE HERE?

"Thy will be done." To whom are you speaking when you state this hallowed phrase? Be always aware that you are speaking to your Self, for you and your Maker cannot be separated. Where do you draw the line between the sunbeam and the sun? Yes, as a ray of Light, as a focus of Consciousness, as an intelligent being that arises from Infinite Intelligence, you can find your way quite well in this world and beyond. But why would you choose to walk alone, unguided, when the One who sees all, knows all, and loves all is always available to guide your every step?

It is only when you act as an impudent child and demand your independence that you encounter difficulties, but God is infinitely patient with his offspring. He allows you to find your own way, and if you should become lost and cry out for help, he responds. But do not wait until the road is bumpy or you get lost. Relinquish this egoic need for independence. Acknowledge and rejoice in your oneness with Spirit. Declare in every moment, "Thy will be done." Then watch how the road smoothes out and spreads out beautifully before you … a golden pathway lighted by the blinding light of the Father, who always knows what is best for his children.

March 11

FEAST ON LOVE

So many of you hunger … you hunger for friendship. You hunger for peace. You hunger for love. You walk around as if you were a starving person, picking up crumbs of what you hunger for wherever you find them, ever grateful to those who drop them.

Open your eyes! The crumbs are infinitesimally small compared to the banquet … the veritable feast of peace, joy, and love which is set and awaiting your enjoyment. The key to this dining room lies within the mind. With your thoughts you create the platters. With your thoughts you create the steaming dishes. With your thoughts you create the knives and forks, and with your thoughts you unlock the doors.

Do you understand the analogy? The mind is the key! Nothing outside of you is real. You create the feast, just as you create the famine. Do you wish to have more love, joy, and peace? Create it, radiate it, and then feast upon it. Do not search and scrounge for crumbs outside of yourself. Be that which you seek, and never again go hungry.

March 12

WHEN TRAGEDY STRIKES

You see the images of tragedy on your television screens. They bring pain to your heart. Why is this? Why do you identify so strongly with the pain of others? It is quite simple: you are viewing a reflection of yourself. Each human is but a mirror of your soul, for there is only one Self.

As above, so below. All human beings are cells in the Body of God. This, my friends, is the meaning of "oneness." Just as the body of the human has its various parts which take on differing appearances, the Body of God, in the form of humanity, does have differing appearances in its varying parts, but all are part of the one Body.

Do you see now why you hurt when others are injured or pass from this life? Some tragedies result in the mass transition of many souls. To you, who see not the big picture, a mass casualty is as a massive wound to your very body. Yes, of course it hurts to see these images … to think of the pain suffered by so many. And why does it hurt? Because, oh Spirit-beings, *it is your body*. There is only one Body.

So, for now you hurt, but does not the body have the most miraculous way of healing? This wound will mend. Healing will take place, and healing of the souls of those left behind will take place even faster as the Body of Man realizes that those who did transition to the other side are not gone forever, but live forever, for all cells in the Body of God are but eternal souls.

March 13

AT YOUR VERY CORE

Carry on your tasks of the day as if nothing were wrong. "But how can I do this," you ask, "when around me my world is falling apart?" Do you see the angst you create with this very thought? It is there you place your focus, and in this way do you perpetuate the crumbling of your circumstances.

Realize that thoughts create things. Shift your focus to the Perfection inside you. This is where peace begins. Radiate that peace outward, knowing that you cannot experience peace without, until peace reigns in your thoughts. So rein in your thoughts. They do not control you—although this fallacy you may have accepted. Throw out such lunacy and take control of your life.

You are perfection at your very core. See this, believe this, and then begin to create this around you. Banish your fears. Know that all things are possible when you tap into the limitless potential of the mind. Mind not what others may have told you throughout your life. Mind not what falsehoods you have believed. Know now that a loving God governs all things … is all things … and when you tap into that Love which lies at your very core, all things are possible—even peace in the midst of seeming chaos. Chaos does not exist at the level of the spirit. Go there to find Peace. Go there to find Love. Go there to find your Self.

March 14

AFTERSHOCKS

The earth shakes and trembles in the aftermath of an even larger quake. "Aftershocks" you do call these, and while they frighten, they are not as shocking as the initial force, for eyes have been opened to the possibility of "more to come." You have a shocking experience in your life, and this in your mind creates the idea that more of the same is possible. Until your eyes were opened, you did not see what could manifest. Once opened, Potential expresses itself again and again.

We use an earthquake as an example, but understand that you have a powerful Force inside of you at your disposal. The very Power of Creation rests within your mind. This Power is fueled by love, and since there is nothing more powerful than that which arises from your Creator, do you see how very powerful you are?

Awaken to the power of Love and to your creative potential. Once awakened, go forth and create aftershocks of love within your world. Be a loving, healing force among those who have not yet awakened.

March 15

ONE TRUE SELF

All of you are so very interconnected. You breathe the very air that has circulated through billions of bodies, yet it is with the spirit that you are even more closely entwined. Where do you draw the boundary between two focuses of Consciousness? Is it at the perimeter which you call skin and bone? This is an artificial border. Just as the borders of your nations are naught but arbitrary lines drawn by governments, the physical body is an artifice.

You are not the body. The physical body cannot contain the Real You. As a spirit-being, you extend into infinity, you live into eternity. And so, we ask you, where is your border? Where do you end, and where does your neighbor begin? You flow into each other. Your every thought affects each other. So love thy neighbor as yourself, for there is only one True Self.

March 16

VAST AND UNLIMITED

There are many fish in the ocean … creatures of many sizes and shapes. Some are dangerous, some benign. These fish are analogous with your thoughts. They swim through your mind –some dangerous, in that they can cause harm to self and to others; some benign, in that they can do good in your world. But just as the fish in the sea are not part of the sea, your thoughts are not you. They are merely visitors, passing through.

You *are* the sea, vast and unlimited … Consciousness flowing without end. With the Mind you gather together the fish into little schools and send them on their way to affect other waves in the ocean, but again: these fish are not the ocean. Your thoughts are not you. You are Pure Consciousness … Pure Love.

What will you do with this knowledge?

March 17

WATCHING BEAUTY UNFOLD

Beauty abounds, if you would only open your eyes. Beauty is, indeed, in the eye of the beholder. What is beauty to one person—and yes, even to one culture—may not be considered beauty to another. All of life is like this—subject to perceptions and beliefs. Each individual focus of consciousness sees their current reality from a different perspective based solely on their state of consciousness. The higher the state, the more beautiful the perceptions.

Believe us when we tell you that it is possible to look upon all creations and see beauty. If you do not yet perceive this, then you have yet work to do … lessons to learn. But fret not, for what could be more beautiful than watching beauty unfold as you work to unfold your own consciousness bit by loving bit? Blessings to you in this beautiful journey you call Life.

March 18

WHAT YOU DO BEST

Share your talents with the world.
In this way you do heal
The pain that others suffer
As God's gifts you do reveal.

Each one has some ability
Which they are meant to share
And they can help to heal the world
If share them it they do dare.

What talents were you given?
What is it you do best?
In what way can you thus serve
By sharing with the rest?

It's where you find your passion
That true service you can give.
For in this way you blossom
And help others best to live.

So search inside for your true skills
The ones that make you sing.
If used then to enhance your world
True peace and love you'll bring.

March 19

A FRESH START

Each day is a fresh start. As you open your eyes, think not back upon what has gone before, but rejoice in yet another opportunity to create anew. If you find yourself filled with worry, then you are holding onto false illusions of yourself and the situations around you. Surrender!

You, as a limited self (as the ego would have you believe you are), are not in charge. As you open your eyes each day, give thanks that your eyes have been opened, and give this day to your Highest Self.

There is a power with infinite intelligence and infinite love which has chosen you to express Itself. Use this power to create a beautiful day for yourself.

No worries, my friend.

March 20

BASK IN THE FREEDOM

Bury your resentments. They do you only harm, keeping you from expressing your true nature. So many of you hold onto negative emotions as if they were your friends—as if you could not survive without them. Hear us now: You would thrive without them.

It is only the survival instinct of the ego which has convinced you that you must maintain your separation and supposed superiority over others. This is primitive, instinctual behavior. Rise above resentment to the level of love and unity. Should the ego feel threatened, so be it. Love is all that matters.

As you nurture the spirit—by loving instead of judging—the ego's strong grip begins to loosen. Bid it farewell. You have paid the price for its dominance; now bask in the freedom of letting your spirit soar.

March 21

THE GRAND STRATEGY

Strategy is a word you use for a detailed plan. Do you not realize that your Creator has a strategy for you? You are to awaken however slowly to the Truth that you are not merely a human being, but a being far more powerful—a spirit-being … a child of God temporarily clothed in a human body with arms and legs and a brain so as to formulate and carry out strategies of your own.

It is part of the Grand Strategy that many do not realize who and what they are. This makes the Adventure all the more grand as the children of God help each other to awaken by leading by example. Those who have awakened exude such love and compassion that it is impossible not to see and feel Spirit as their very being.

An interesting strategy, is it not? Where do you fit in the Plan? Will you awaken fully or remain deluded? It is yet another part of the Grand Strategy that you are given the choice.

How will you choose?

March 22

THE ONE ETERNAL TRUTH

Truth is an elusive thing, for in your reality all is based upon perception, and perception is different from every angle. What is blue to you may not be the same as blue to your brother, yet how would you know? So often you do insist that your truth is the only one, but again we ask you: how would you know?

There is one Truth which never changes, no matter what the angle of perception. That Truth is, I AM. Truth is not found in "You are," for how do you know what "you" is? You cannot. "I" never changes. The "I" of "I AM" is eternal and unchanging, and what is the greatest Truth of all, then—worthy of celebration and veneration—that you are that very I AM.

How can we know this with certainty? "We" cannot, but the I AM can and does know this. All who recognize I AM within themselves recognize this fundamental Truth. Celebrate your I-AM-ness today by seeing the I AM in all that is.

March 23

SAVIORS

Saviors come in many forms. Yes, some walk in a human body and teach lessons which last for millennia, but saviors need not become known to millions to have an effect. A savior is one who opens your eyes to the Truth of Who You Are. In this way, a savior could be one with whom you live, a friend, or even a passing stranger who makes a comment or perhaps glows in such a way that you see an Essence there that is unmistakable. You recognize in those beings a part of yourself. You finally realize that that glow—that Essence—is Who You Are as well.

And why are these mirrors of yourself your saviors? Because, dear ones, they save you from spending yet another moment living with the false belief that you are not connected to every other soul by your very essence—by your light. Shine brightly today and save someone yourself.

March 24

FLOAT IN THIS SEA

Scattered thoughts run about the mind as if at random. Pay them no heed. The brain wants to chatter incessantly, but beyond the brain lies your connection with All That Is—with the very Source of those thoughts which run here and there. Do not eschew those thoughts, for they, like all things, are holy. Simply let them run their course and place your focus on nothingness, knowing that where seemingly there is nothing, there is, in fact, contained the Seed of All.

Spend time in this sea of "nothingness," for it contains the greatest creative potential. Out of it arise those thoughts which run about. Out of it arose you. Float in this sea for a while each day and give thanks. Your gratitude is much appreciated, for in giving thanks you acknowledge the Source of your ability to give thanks.

OF THE WHOLE

Wish upon a falling star …
Guess the number in a jar …
All seems haphazard, nothing sure.
Is nothing certain evermore?

Yes, one truth stands o'er the rest.
Of time and doubt it does pass the test:
You come from Spirit – know this now.
Into your heart this Truth allow.

The stars you see come from this Source.
All arises from the sacred Force.
The birds, the trees, the glistening dew …
The plants and animals, yes, and you.

There's nothing out there you do see
That does not come from Energy.
Inseparable, then, are you from All.
From all God made, both big and small.

Know this as you walk today.
See your world in this new way.
Feel how important is your role
As part and parcel of The Whole.

March 26

THE DEPTHS OF YOUR SOUL

Just as a pebble sinks to the bottom of a lake, your conscious mind sinks into the depths of the Pure Consciousness of which it is a part. Deeper and deeper you go as you relax the body and allow the thoughts to drift away on the surface. There in the depths will you find peace—away from the vagaries of the winds and currents. There in the depths will you find silence. It may seem dark, but in actuality, it is filled with Light ... not brightness such as that radiated by your sun, but brightness within your very soul that has been there all along, waiting for you to leave the surface with its constant changes and rest a while in the peaceful depths.

While there you may ask, "Fill me with your light." When this request is answered, then you will know what true brightness is, and why—in your limited language—you do equate love and light. Words are, indeed, limited, for no artifice of man can describe that which is limitless. It can only be known through experience. Visit the depths of your soul, leaving the surface of your physical world for a while on a regular basis, and words will no longer be necessary.

CLEAR THE FROST

Frost on the window
Obscures the view
So thick at times
No light can get through.

But take a finger
And wipe a small hole.
Peer inside
And lo! There's the soul!

What icy exterior
Does obscure what's inside?
Why so much
From your True Self do you hide?

Take a large cloth
And clear the whole pane.
Never more hide the light
Not from frost, fog, or rain.

The light that's inside
Is just waiting to shine...
To show the whole world
That what's there is Divine.

So with your heart and your mind
Clear away what obscures
The light inside, yes, your spirit ...
The part of you that endures.

March 28

THERE IS ONLY NOW TO LOVE

Forget the past. It was a moment of the present that is no longer present and no longer affects you unless you hold onto it so tightly that you fail to see the beauty in the present moment. Yes, certainly you can learn from those past moments, but not by dwelling there. Take the lessons of how you could have reacted to those now-passed-moments and apply that learning in the present-now-moment. If you were not loving, be loving now. If you were loving, be ever more so. Do you get the picture?

The only thing that matters is love, for love is what you are—pure Spirit in human form. It is your mission now to express your True Self. You do not do that in the past. You do not do that in moments not yet here. You do that now, followed by now, followed by now. There is only now to be the Presence of Love. It is quite simple, especially when not bogged down by thoughts of now-moments-passed. Begin anew in each now-moment to express your Self, and there will be no need to look back, for your only reality will be one of perfecting Love and loving Perfection.

March 29

SOLDIER ON

You look upon the covers of your magazines in a store and feel discouragement. So many are drawn to pictures of weapons or to improving exterior appearances. So few seem drawn to things of the Spirit. "Where are the magazines touting love and charity?" The consciousness of humanity as a whole has not risen sufficiently to create a reality in which interest in Truth supersedes the gifts of instant gratification of the flesh and mortal mind.

Does this mean that you should surrender your efforts to help to raise the consciousness of those around you? Far from it. Soldier on. Radiate love at all times, even to those who seem most closed off from their Spirit-nature. You do not realize the full impact of your love at this time, but that does not mean that you should stop loving. Work only on raising your own consciousness. In so doing, you are building up the whole, for all is One.

March 30

THE FRUITS OF LIFE

Berries on a branch
Hang heavy and low.
The fruit of the tree
So abundant does it grow.

You reach up and pluck it.
It's there for you to take.
With all of this sweetness,
Just what will you make?

All the world is yours,
Just like the tree that's filled with fruit.
Yet so many wander blindly
And fail to see this Truth.

See the branches full,
Or see the tree stripped bare.
What you see is your experience;
What you think, it appears there.

Will your cup be empty?
Or will you choose to see it full?
The world is as you make it:
A gentle push or mighty pull.

Make the choice to see all goodness,
For Goodness is your Source.
Demonstrate That which you are
And never more will you need force.

There is power in surrender.
There is might in being still.
All the fruits of Life await you
When you surrender to God's will.

March 31

BEYOND WORDS

Words limit your description of the Self. By choosing a particular word you either limit your concept of who you are, or you expand it, but never can a limited word—no matter how expressive—express the beauty, glory, and grandeur of the True Self.

Because you rely so much on words instead of feelings—instead of sheer experience—you limit your experience of Spirit. Sit in a quiet space and allow the words which pass through your mind to drift away. Ask to be filled with the Presence of Love. Breathe deeply and simply be that Presence. Tune in to your heart. Repeat this process day after day and there will come a day when you will have an experience far beyond words. Then you will know what true Love is, and what you have always been, and will always be ... beyond words.

April 1

YOUR ONGOING EVOLUTION

Hirsute and unintelligible, the early forms of man did wander the earth much like the animals in the jungle, concerned primarily with survival. Now clothed and well fed, you have institutions in place which virtually ensure your security and survival from day to day. Evolution is a good thing, and like you, yourself, evolution is eternally ongoing.

You as a human being are evolving just as you as a spirit-being are evolving. No longer unintelligible, you can express your thoughts. Do you realize that how you express them determines the very rate of your evolution? You can remain at the level of the primates and throw stones, or you can rise to new levels and throw olive branches.

Forgiveness, compassion, and empathy are advanced attributes of the human-being, but innate attributes of the Spirit. Express your True Self at all times and rise above.

April 2

WHOLLY HOLY

See yourself as perfection, not as an imperfect body. Allow the healing energy that creates the universe to be you, to flow through you, and to enliven you. You need not always run to doctors who practice their craft by fixing what is broken—by putting a patch on a symptom. Know yourself, instead, as whole and holy, then ask for this holiness to permeate all of your cells. Focus only on your holiness and health, and draw the healing energy through you.

Do this every day to banish the thought that you are less than whole … less than perfect. Ask that God's will and yours be perfectly matched. Know in your heart that God is Perfection, and as a creation of the Creator, know that you are Perfection as well. Knowing this, draw that Perfection through the body and be healed.

GIVE OF YOUR SELF

By helping others do you grow.
In this way true love you show.
You set aside the self a while
And help another soul to smile.

To volunteer your time is great.
Some may say you are a saint.
But let it not go to your head,
The many things that may be said.

You know inside that what you do
Comes back again to affect you.
What goes to others bounces back.
When much you give, you feel no lack.

To volunteer of time and self
Is to discover newfound wealth.
It shows you a new way to think
When with another you forge a link.

So ask yourself, what is your gift
That you can use to give a lift.
And in this way impact the whole
By sharing what's inside your soul.

April 4

BEAUTY IN THE SILENCE

Silence is the order of the day. Speak little and listen for once. Hear what others have to say. Hear the voices in your head. Hear the beating of your heart. All around you information sings, yet so often you do not hear it as you jump to put in the next word. Pay not so much attention to the words you can create, but to the voices that come at you in your thoughts and from those around you. There are many lessons to be learned by silencing your own vocalizations and simply listening.

Give the voice a break for a day and see what you can learn. When you do not answer a comment immediately or instantly offer your own opinion, you create opportunities. When you do not fill the silence with endless chatter, you clear the mind for inspiration. Become a clear canvas. Allow Spirit to paint new impressions instead of the same worn picture. Beauty arises from fresh starts.

Hear us well: There is beauty in the silence. Mute your voice for a day and see what Spirit has to say.

April 5

MIRRORS

Look into a stranger's eyes, and what do you see there? Look closely and you can see your own reflection. You have heard it said that the eyes are the mirror of the soul, and this is true—but not because you see an actual reflection of yourself on the surface. It is because you see there the self-same emotions and attributes that all spirit-beings share.

A smile or a frown can change the entire face, but the eyes hide nothing. Deep pools with bottomless depth, they hold the mystery of the Universe. Look into a mirror and peer quite closely into your own eyes. Who and what do you see there? Look even closer ... There in that liquid base is the sea of all possibility. Those eyes can hold great sorrow as well as great love. All of Life lies there. Yes, in there lies the soul—the same as in your fellow spirit-beings.

Which aspect of your being will you express today? Dive in deep to find the love that is always there in you and others. Do your best to bring it to the surface. Leave nothing hidden.

April 6

IN ALL THINGS

Where is God in times of trouble? God is the loving gesture from a friend … the gentle touch upon an arm that says, "You are not alone." God is in the gathering of loved ones to give each other strength. God is in the beauty of a flower that catches your eye in your greatest moment of sorrow to let you know that life goes on and beauty continues.

You are never alone, for God dwells within you as Spirit. Call upon the Spirit within to awaken and fill your heart. If you do not feel it immediately, Spirit will send you messengers in the form of a kiss from a puppy, a casserole from a neighbor, a kind word from a passing stranger. These are not mere accidents … this is God expressing Itself as Love … the true nature of all things.

April 7

BLESSINGS

You tell others to count their blessings. What is a blessing, but the awareness of goodness in your life. Do you not realize that you are the blessing? Life is the blessing. All that you see and all that you have is a blessing. You would lose count, were you to spend your day counting your blessings when you see each day from the viewpoint of Spirit.

You are Spirit. Therefore, see each moment as a blessing. Practice being the spirit-being that you are, and walk about this day bestowing blessings upon all you encounter. How do you do this? Radiate blessings with your thoughts and know that they are being received, whether or not they are acknowledged.

You are a blessing. Use your full power as a spirit-being to share your Self with your fellow spirit-beings. Bless all that is, and blessings be upon you.

April 8

ONE CONSCIOUSNESS

There is only one Consciousness… one Mind. All is a vibration of the one Consciousness. This is why you read of a spectrum of consciousness. There is only variety in vibration of the One Divine Mind. The body identified with your spirit is imbued with the Consciousness that resonates perfectly with your individualized focus of the Divine Mind. These are the so-called Consciousness Units.

When you see another body, it is not separate from you, for there is only One Mind. It is merely a higher or lower vibration than yours, but not separate—simply different vibrations along the same continuum.

All that you see with your eyes … you are That. Inseparable. That other body? You are That. That other mind? You are That. Can you separate colors? They appear different, but what are colors but the same effect of light along a spectrum—a continuum of energy. You are That. Inseparable from All That Is. Travel the spectrum and experience your Self.

April 9

BLINDFOLDS

All around you are angels. Do you think the world consists only of that which you see? You are swimming in a sea of vibrating energy, but, my friends, you are that very energy. We cannot expect you to understand that which is beyond your current ability to perceive, but we do wish for you to open your minds to the possibilities beyond your current perceptions.

Why would you wish to remain blindfolded if you knew that by simply having the courage to remove your blindfold there would be revealed new wonders, new opportunities, and new beginnings? Begin by asking yourself which of your beliefs do limit you, then grab a tiny corner of your blindfold and lift it ever so slightly. The light that reveals itself in doing so is just a beginning. Now you can choose to rip off the blindfold or remove it bit by bit. It matters not the speed. Do so at your comfort, for all will be revealed as the light of love pours through you and from you.

April 10

ALL IS REAL

A manifestation of the Life Force—God—that is what you are, and that is what all things are, for all things are Spirit. Whether in your thoughts, your mind's visions, or before your very eyes, all is a manifestation of Consciousness. So, is a spirit-guide real if you see this guide in your mind's eye with tall feather and stripes upon the face? It is as real as a flower you hold in your hand, for all things … all things … are formed by the movement of consciousness by the One Divine Mind. All things are merely different vibrations along the spectrum of consciousness.

The One Divine Mind created you, and you, as a manifestation of that Mind, go on to create yet more manifestations. Some take form, and some do not, but as you are not separate from that Mind, then all is of the One Consciousness. So, what is real and what is imagination? There is no difference, my friend. All, including you, are creations of the Mind.

So, how will you use these creations? If you use them for your soul's growth, if you use them to be more loving, more "God-like," then God will be well pleased.

April 11

FOCUS

A treasure trove of gifts awaits you.
You merely need to ask.
To trust in all Creation,
This is your greatest task.

The world is ripe for picking.
The fullest low-hung fruit
Becomes yours for the taking
When your trust is absolute.

From where does come this bounty?
From where does it arise?
The answer, when you know your Self
Will come as no surprise...

The mind creates all that you see,
Whether good or whether tragic.
It happens when you focus thought.
It's not what you'd call magic.

All that is good comes from the Spirit.
It's man who does abuse
The power given to him
When loving thoughts he does refuse.

So be careful what you wish for.
Good advice in every case,
For as a co-creator
You affect the human race.

April 12

WHAT GOOD IS A FRIEND?

What good is a friend, if you love them not? A friend is one you practice upon—one with whom you practice patience, kindness, compassion, and non-judgment. You would wish them to display the same towards you, but that is not always the case. And that, my friend, is the value of a friend. When they display their humanness and at times are not as loving to you as you would wish, it is those times that remind you that your friend exists not to please you and make you feel good. Your friend exists to mirror your Self ... to give back to you by giving you opportunities to love them for themselves and in spite of themselves.

With this definition in mind, is not the whole world a potential friend? Make friends with all you see, for all you see are merely mirrors of the greater Self, all experiencing themselves in human form. So when others do something that is utterly human, you can say to them, "It is all right, my friend. I know Who you are, and I love you all the more for it."

April 13

MIRACLES

You wait for miracles, yet what is a miracle? It is something so outside the ordinary that you think it impossible ... a special healing ... an apparition ... If these are miracles, then miracles happen all the time. You become so entrained to the lower vibrations of human limitations that you fail to see that you are a miracle-maker yourself. Take off your chains. Remove the thoughts that hold you back from performing the impossible. Do you wish to fly? Man wished to fly, and now he does so with machines he has created—a miracle to those who lived years ago. Do you wish to fly without machines? Experience yourself as the spirit-being that you are and move with great freedom in your dreams.

Remove your shackles and dream. What will be your next miracle? You are limited only by your thoughts.

April 14

NO MYSTERY

Mystery schools ... providing ancient teachings from eras past ... Do you not see the similarities in the messages from school to school? And the messages come to you now from the unseen world, unchanged: There is but one Mind guiding all that is, bringing order where otherwise there would be chaos, through the application of immutable laws of Nature.

Cause and effect ... all is linked ... nothing happens by chance, most especially not you. You are not an accident. Your experience here is quite deliberate, and yes, God knows every hair that grows on your head. This is a mystery to you. "How can it be, in a world with billions of beings, that God would know of my every breath?"

It is because, beloved child, you are a child of that God ... the Infinite Living Mind. What is infinite knows all without mystery, but what is finite must be satisfied to trust and know that all is in perfect order always.

April 15

RESURRECTION

Resurrection … you know this as a rising from the dead, but what is it that arises? It is the spirit, which has never died, and can never die. The body and all physical matter are ephemeral. Yes, material things experience death, but you are not a material object. You are temporarily experiencing your current reality through an apparatus called the body, but what is it that is doing the experiencing? It is Spirit—that which you are.

All experience resurrection. All arise from the dead, for all were never the body to begin with. All spirit is eternal and continues evolving ever upward for all of eternity. Resurrection is but a process … not unique, not miraculous, but part of the ongoing process of Life.

April 16

YOUR DAILY SUPPLEMENT

Do you tire of hearing the same messages here each day? Do the words begin to repeat themselves? If so, then why do you return to repeat the experience? It is quite simple. Yours is a world of many low vibrations. These messages of love and oneness … these messages from Spirit and of Spirit carry a much higher vibration. The very act of reading them does raise your own vibration and bring good feelings and harmony.

These words are as a pill you take each day. If you were to stop taking these vibrational vitamins, all the more difficult would it be to remain positive and loving in a world filled with so much pain and darkness. While it is not mandatory to take your vitamins, when such aid is available, is it not sensible to partake of it? This, your daily dose of love, is filled with the very vibration of its Source. Partake of it freely—this spiritual supplement—and know that you are loved greatly.

April 17

YOUR INNER GLOW

Sitting on a park bench, you watch the mass of humanity pass by. So many different sizes, shapes, and manners of dressing ... All seem so very different from you, but what if you could see beyond the exterior? What if that which causes your first impressions were not there? Would all look the same? Indeed, even with the spirit body there are differences, but when seen with the eyes of Spirit, these subtle differences matter not. What you would see is a glow. This glow is quite bright in some and dim in others. Some glow in vibrant colors, whilst others lack such vibrancy.

Do you yet understand that this glow is a reflection of your True Self ... made up of all of your beliefs and emotions? In the spirit world, the Self cannot be hidden. It is there for all to see. The beauty of the more evolved souls is so attractive that those who have not yet evolved as far want nothing less than to grow to that point. There is no deception—no desire or need for it. Only you in your world think that you can hide behind your disguises, but never for long. Come out from behind your veils and let your True Self shine in such a way that you serve as a model for others who remain yet in darkness.

April 18

ON MEDITATION

Sitting quietly by a river,
The leaves go floating by…
This is how to still the brain
And see with your mind's eye.

Begin with some deep breathing.
Follow the air as it does flow.
Then as your thoughts come to your mind
Release them – let them go.

The brain will want to chatter.
To stop it do not try.
Acknowledge that it works for you,
Then let the thoughts float by.

You may wish to choose a mantra,
A word that brings you peace.
Then say this word repeatedly,
Quite slowly without cease.

It's in the silence of the gaps
Between each word you say
That you enter God's great kingdom
And in His world do play.

No words can match this feeling.
It is different for each one.
But once you taste the nectar
To God's side you'll want to run.

But there's no need for rushing.
God will walk with you each second.
Long after you resume your day
For His help you clearly beckoned.

Such an awakening is yours, my friend.
Such gifts they do await.
For taking time to sit in peace –
For taking time to meditate.

In this way you show commitment.
You set your priorities quite right.
You tell the Spirit, "You are first,
Please fill me with Your light."

And so it is when you do ask.
Your life is meant for this:
To know your oneness with Creation
To taste the glory of God's bliss.

April 19

PAVLOV'S PEOPLE

The jingle of a bell causes repeated actions in a well-trained dog. "Pavlovian responses" you do call these, but are humans not so well trained? Do you not respond robotically, as if programmed, to such a wide variety of stimuli? Do you not believe that it is mandatory to respond in a certain way to certain types of news and to certain ideas?

Does the untrained dog salivate automatically at the sound of a bell? What do you do automatically in response to so many things in your life? The tone of a voice … the pushing of a certain button … do these often not cause you to react in ways far worse than salivating? Yet all the more real do your reactions affect your physical body from these learned responses. We ask you today for awareness. Keep track of how many times you do "salivate" and what are your "ringing bells." You may be quite enlightened at the discoveries. Seek true enlightenment by uncovering the falsehoods which keep you from expressing your true loving nature.

April 20

PAIN AND PERCEPTION

Pain comes to every human. It is a vital aspect of life in the physical world. How one person reacts to pain may differ from another. This you call a "threshold," reflecting one's tolerance for pain. Some can take very little, and others seemingly quite a lot. Why the difference? Life is about the experiences, and what each person—each soul—learns from these experiences. If all had the same pain threshold, there would not be so much learning, but it is not necessary to suffer in order to learn.

You can learn simply by taking control of your thoughts, and in this way raise your threshold to such a degree that what previously may have pained you no longer affects you at all. A miracle, you say? Not at all. Simply the learning of another lesson. Pain is not necessary. Tolerance goes up and down for a reason. May you suffer little, having learned well that pain begins with perception.

April 21

PERFECTION

Perfection is not possible whilst in physical form. Does this mean you should not seek it? Of course not. Your task in life is to develop your divinity … to perfect your expression as the presence of Love, as a co-creator with the Creator, that Infinite Living Mind which is Perfection itself, and All Possibilities itself.

Within All Possibilities exists imperfection, does it not? So berate yourself not when you express imperfection, but recognize that perfection is the highest expression of The All. Recognize that there is always room for improvement. Go easy on yourself with the criticism, but push yourself—gently, always—in the direction of Perfection, knowing it is that Light which attracts you toward such lofty goals in the first place.

April 22

WHEN THINGS SEEM TO PILE UP

Is not death a normal part of life? Are not accidents common events? Does not the body break down? "Yes, but why so many at once?" you ask, when things seem to pile up. Because, my friend, all things in life occur in cycles. All things respond to the Law of Rhythm. Like a pendulum swinging out, then returning to its starting place over and over, all things in Life occur in a rhythmic, cyclical fashion, and these rhythms occur on the micro as well as the macro scale.

Examine anything in your world and you will find the Law of Rhythm … your seasons, your tides, your very moods. Do they not come in waves? Within families, the individual members will experience waves in which there is no sickness, there are no accidents, and no deaths, followed by periods in which these do occur—these natural events of life seen by you as tragedies, but seen by us in the spirit world as periods of growth.

Now see these individual families (the micro, you might say) as members of one larger family known as your neighborhood or town. This larger family (the macro, you might say) may experience the swing of the pendulum in which more than the usual so-called tragic events occur. Follow the pendulum's swing and you will be able to see that calm will follow. Whilst chaos seems to reign, you will see the many ways in which the God Force is at work in this larger family. You will see individuals sharing love in abundance. You will see healing.

Take this analogy even further and see the cycles occurring in the larger family of nations and within humanity as a whole, forever giving you opportunities to express love. It is merely the Law of Rhythm in action. See the cycles and accept what comes and goes with love.

April 23

IN THE FLOW

Things do not turn out as you wish. "But I prayed for this!" you cry. "I wanted it so badly! Why were my prayers not answered?" If you could hear the prayers of the tiny ant at your feet, praying for the strength to climb the hill before it, would you help the ant over the hill if you could see the ant eater lying in wait on the other side?

You do not ever have the big picture. There is always a greater Reality, and the Infinite Living Mind is always at work, orchestrating, guiding, loving . . .

When things do not go as you wish, relax. Could it be that some obstruction lies beyond the next hill, and not the treasure you imagine? When you find yourself going in a new direction, know that when you accept that all is in perfect order always, it is ever so much easier to simply go with the flow. To get into the flow, realize that you are Spirit first and foremost, and that without the Great Spirit you would not even breathe. Strive to bring your will into harmony with that of Spirit, and then you will experience how the flow of life becomes far easier.

April 24

LET THERE BE LIGHT

Why do you speak of God as "Light"? Why do you wish others "love and light"? What is light, but energy—vibrant energy which dispels darkness, revealing Presence. Does not light allow you to see what before you did not realize was there? Does it not bring warmth and comfort? Are these all not qualities of that which you know as God?

When we speak of the "light within," know that you carry these same qualities of brightness, warmth, and comfort within your very being. That light is always present. It is the very fuel which gives you life. If you feel enveloped in darkness, you need only ask to see the light, to feel the light. Focus then on your heart and ask fervently for the light to be revealed. In the asking, with this heart-felt intention and desire, you are your own fire-starter.

Allow your light to shine forth so that you may serve as a beacon of God's love to all with whom you deal. Blessings be upon you this day as you shine your light upon the world.

April 25

DIVINE ATTRIBUTES

Depravity. This is what you call aberrant behavior in which human beings commit atrocities, such as taking the life of another in a particularly gruesome way. "How can this happen if there is a loving God which rules the universe?" you ask.

It happens, my friends, because God does not rule in a manner liken unto a king who gives orders or takes away liberties. God is the Infinite Loving Mind which brings order out of chaos. Man is liken unto God in that the human being has a mind as well, and is free to act, to think, to love, and to develop those aspects of himself which reflect his True Self.

If a man did not realize he had all of the attributes of the Divine Mind, he would not know to use those attributes for only good. He would seek power by using his mind in ways contrary to his True Nature, and this you do see in your headlines each day. You view this with great distress, but we ask you to view this man-made chaos as the creation of those who do not recognize Who and What they are. They have not heeded the subtle calling of the spirit, and thus remain blindfolded.

To find peace in a world of blinded souls, remove your own blindfold and send forth emanations that reflect Truth. In other words, be loving to all creatures and all of creation—to all of Life—for you are Love itself.

April 26

SPECIAL TOUCHES

Belly rubs. Back rubs. Foot massages. Why are these so special? It is more than just the human touch, which is special enough in and of itself. These special moments of sharing form a bond—a connection—soul to soul. "I care for you," they say. "I know how good this feels, and I wish for you to feel good and to feel my love." This is Spirit speaking through touch, using the body as the expression of love that it is, and isn't it beautiful?

Have you touched another in a special way lately? Have you gone beyond the hug or kiss—which are special indeed—and have you shown tenderness and caring through a caress? This kind of action—this connection—speaks silently and speaks volumes, for the spirit need not speak at all when it speaks the language of love through touch. Touch another with love, and give voice to your soul.

April 27

ORDER, NOT DISORDER

Your doctors speak of those with a "multiple personality disorder." To the one who experiences this so-called "disorder," are they not experiencing life as if through multiple minds? How do you think that the Great Infinite Mind experiences Life? Is it through its One Mind or through the billions of minds which that Great Spirit has manifested?

Hear us well: There is no difference. Is there not one mind (with a small "m") guiding the diverse minds of the one experiencing multiple personalities? Do you see now how there can be One Mind guiding all of the minds which it has manifested? It is only a matter of scale.

It is difficult for one small mind to control more than one personality, and this oft causes problems, but the One Divine Mind is omnipotent. What is infinite has no limitations.

There is only One Mind. That which thinks itself separate and individual is but a focus of the One Mind that is focusing too greatly on its small self. Could it not be seen as an "individual personality disorder" to suffer under the illusion that you are limited, separate, and unloved? There could be no greater illusion. Multiple personalities … One Loving Mind bringing order to all. It is quite simple.

April 28

FENCES

Picket fences … slats of wood lined side by side to form a barrier. This forms not an impenetrable barrier, simply a visible sign of demarcation … a sign that says to all that what lies on one side of this fence is mine and on the other, yours. Yes, such fences are quite pretty, but at the same time they do mark your so-called territory.

You have many picket fences in your world … your clothing, your words, your facial expressions … none of them impenetrable, but all of them ways of showing, "Stand back. Keep some distance. This is my territory."

You had a famous leader who asked another to "Take down this wall," and in so doing, were not the barriers between nations removed? What walls have you erected around yourself? Are they tall brick walls or picket fences with tiny gaps through which you allow your light to shine?

Take down your walls. Pull down your picket fences. Give yourself fully to your fellow man. Show your love without false barriers. What good does a picket fence do? It is only for show. Show the world Who you are.

April 29

SUFFER NOT

Suffer not, my children, for all experiences are temporary. Can you not endure a bit of discomfort, knowing that light always arises from the darkness? Do not wallow there in the muck. It may seem easy to become stuck when this becomes a familiar place, but look within your heart and find there the way out of that which holds you down.

This light inside will guide you, even if for now it is but a tiny pinprick. Follow it. Hang onto it as you would a life preserver, for is that not what Spirit is? The Great Life Preserver? The Preserver of love … the Preserver of your very consciousness.

Break out of the darkness, knowing it is but a temporary place you visit so that you can once again revel in the light when you actively seek it.

April 30

COLOR YOUR WORLD

The sky appears blue, but is it really this color? What is color, but different vibrations along the spectrum of light? You vibrate as well, and your color changes with your thoughts and emotions… at times blue, at times red with anger, at times yellow with fear. Understand that we use these in allegorical fashion, for each color does have a particular frequency which resonates with the energy centers in your body. Red indicates stability …yellow, power … and blue, spiritual understanding. Green is oft associated with love, for it resonates with the heart center, so when you are feeling "blue," imagine a beautiful field of emerald green light surrounding you and filling your heart. Flood your body with this green color until it radiates outward.

It is difficult to be "blue" when bathed in love. Share this love-bath with others who are a bit off-color, and watch the effects. A bit of emotional artistry is a good thing. Today, and every day, color your world with love.

May 1

THE PENDULUM'S SWING

Carousels go round and round.
The horses do go up and down.
Everything in life revolves.
This is how your world evolves.

All does cycle, this you see.
With this knowledge you are free
To worry not, "Will this pain pass?
Or am I stuck in this morass?"

What comes around will pass on by.
To change this, you need not even try,
For rhythm is a law of life.
With cycles all the world is rife.

So when the pendulum swings out
No need to worry or to shout.
It will swing back, of this be sure.
But you need not feel it ever more.

When times are good, enjoy them well
Knowing you can rise above the hell
That happens when the bob swings back
By trying out a different tack …

Rise above it, my dear friend!
Go to that place that has no end.
Know that baser vibes you need not feel
When you ascend where all is real.

Ride the cycle when it's good.
Enjoy your life, of course you should.
But when pain enters, as it will,
Sit in the silence and be still.

There you'll find the peace you seek.
This is when are blessed the meek.
And riding thus the backward swing,
Into your life God peace will bring.

May 2

GOOD VS. EVIL

In a world of duality such as yours, you have what you do know as good and evil. These are both ends of the same spectrum. There are varying degrees of each. Where does good end and evil begin? It is a matter of perception, and perception varies with the perceiver.

When is it justified to rejoice over the death of one who perpetrated evil? We would say that first you must understand that death is only the end of the physical body. You cannot kill the soul. The soul always pays the price for its acts. It is the Law of Cause and Effect.

Is it justified to take the life of another in retaliation for the taking of lives or to stop the taking of yet more lives? You do this for what you call "justice." Know that justice is an act which rides the path between good and evil, sliding the bar toward the center. What is the motive? Always study the motive. If love is behind the act and not power, gain, or glory, there you will find peace. These are difficult choices and thoughts you face in this world of duality, but always you have love as your litmus test.

May 3

MUSHROOMS

Soldiers in a battle—that is what you are. We hesitate to use such bellicose words, but quite appropriate are they in reference to your world of light and dark. So many spend so much time in darkness that it becomes like a home. They grow comfortable there. They feed on it like your mushrooms, growing in darkness amidst the stench. All of these negative images we thrust upon you to awaken your understanding that you can bring light into your world. You need not spread the fungus.

Open the windows wide on those in darkness by shining your light so brightly they cannot fail to see it. At first, those mired in negativity may shield the eyes and rebel, but shine on. Soon they will recognize this long-forgotten feeling. The subconscious knows it as love, the true home. Use love as your weapon in this battle against darkness and shine it like a laser until you help those around you to emerge from their hiding place and find their True Self.

May 4

NOT WITHOUT SOME PAIN

Sounds of creation: creaks and groans
And what at times do sound like moans.
But is it suffering that you hear?
Let us make this perfectly clear …

Does not the mother cry in pain?
When giving birth she moans the same.
For creation is a wondrous thing.
These creaks and groans pure joy do sing.

A bit of pain is worth the cost
To bring again what ne'er was lost—
The presence of spirit to the sight …
Bringing Consciousness to the light.

All is spirit, can't you see?
With this knowledge you are free.
But not without a creak or groan
For suffering's what leads you home.

If you knew only love and peace
You would not ever seek release.
And thus would stagnate your soul's growth
For this your soul did take an oath:

"I promise I will always grow
And do my best true love to show
Even if the cost is high
I will be born and then I'll die."

But just a temporary stint,
For this human life will give a hint
Of your true nature—what is real
Through creaks and groans life will reveal

That all is Spirit—this you'll learn
And then the pain inside you'll spurn.
No longer will you need to moan
For then you truly will be home.

May 5

LOOK STRAIGHT AHEAD

When watching the sun rise over the sea, from anywhere you look upon the –who horizon the sun is straight ahead. How do you explain this miracle? It is quite simple: As above, so below. From anywhere you look, the Source of All Love is straight ahead as well as there within. As without, so within.

Look straight ahead as you walk. Always are you guided. The sun always rises and love is ever present. These are things upon which you can always rely. Look not to the ephemeral, but to that which is eternal: the soul—the seat of Spirit—there within your heart. Feel it and follow it, and never will you go astray.

BELIEVE

Those who believe in miracles do experience them. What is a miracle, but an event or action beyond the normal human experience. Do you not yet understand that there occur events and actions far beyond the human experience at all times? There exist dimensions upon dimensions. All co-exist and inter-mingle, but you are presently blinded by your physical senses to other realities.

Look again at the opening sentence: "Those who believe in miracles do experience them." Belief is the key that unlocks the door to other realms. You create first with thought. If you do not believe there is anything beyond the physical, then you cannot create so-called miraculous experiences for yourself. Stretch your beliefs bit by bit so as not to exceed your comfort zone too much at first.

Believe that your world is not all there is and that you never walk alone. As you then experience tiny "miracles," you can modify your belief system even more and progress from baby steps to giant leaps for mankind.

Miracles are not miraculous. Never do they break the immutable laws of nature. It is simply a fact that Nature is far more expansive than the physical realm. It is your human nature to think your realm is all there is. Take a few baby steps. Take your time. Then, when you are ready, take a giant leap and believe.

May 7

FORGIVENESS … THE GREATEST GIFT

Forgiveness … the greatest gift
When used to heal a painful rift.

Those who harbor hate and anger—
Who hold for others hardened rancor,
Hold within their chest a stone
Leaving them to feel alone.

Yet when you find it in your heart
To heal that which does set you apart,
Then you know the inner peace
That enters with a great release.

It comes when you can finally say,
"I do forgive you on this day."
Forgiveness doesn't say, "You're right."
It doesn't carry power and might.

It's nothing but a touch of grace
That brushes softly 'cross the face
And without judgment says, "I know
That all of us are here to grow.
And if I send you love, not hate,
Then easier will be your fate."

All must pay for what they do.
You face your actions, this is true.
But seeing that we all do err
And showing that the love's still there

Then in this way you show to all
That even those who take a fall
Can walk the straight and narrow path
When met with love instead of wrath.

May 8

RESONANCE

What is resonance, but when two or more waves enjoy compatibility in their frequency. You know a kindred spirit immediately upon meeting one by the very feeling they produce in you. This is resonance. Your energetic signatures—your personal vibrational frequencies—are in tune, not dissonant.

Energy is malleable. It changes in accordance with your thoughts and feelings. This is why your friends may change over time, for the personal vibration does change as one develops spiritually and emotionally. You will find yourself gathering 'round you souls of like vibration.

Is it time to move on when you no longer resonate with one you have known for years? Ask your Self. What is discord, but two frequencies vibrating out of sync. While you may never reach perfect resonance, radiate love. Pure Love is the highest vibration. It brings all others into sync with it.

Synchronize with those around you by being the very presence of love. Do you have such power? Why, of course you do! There is naught but love, and you are it. Even the lesser vibrations come from love, but do reflect an absence of purity. Seek harmony in all facets of your life and be in resonance with All That Is. Raise your vibration with thoughts of love, and harmonize your world.

May 9

TREES VS. FOREST

Hidden in the forest lies the answer to the puzzle. You cannot see the big picture, for you see only details—tiny pieces of the puzzle. One appears to be a great oak tree, and so you think the world is made of oak trees. You step a bit farther along the path and you see a palm tree, and your whole conception of what is true changes. "The world must be made of palm trees, instead!" And you take a step farther around a bend in your path and encounter an elm. "What is this new reality? Am I living in a world of oaks, of palms, or elms?"

My friend, it is true what they say: You cannot see the forest for the trees. Reality is far greater than the individual piece you perceive with your physical senses. Be not deceived. Have faith and trust that all will be revealed in time. For now, do not root your beliefs so firmly in physical perception until you can step fully beyond the forest and fly.

May 10

CHOCOLATES FOR THE SOUL

Chocolates for the soul … little morsels of wisdom that you do collect and digest for the pleasure they bring. Perhaps you keep a small diary of these delectable treats—words which speak to your heart and make it sing … words which remind you that this world of meat and potatoes is not so full of gristle as it seems.

If you do not have your collection of sweet morsels now, we advise you to begin collecting them. There are times when you need a little treat—a pick-me-up to remind you of the path you are on. Chocolates for the soul … you will know them when you find them. Collect them carefully and digest them slowly, savoring every bite. This is how you get through the dark nights.

BARRIERS

Barriers … walls you erect around yourself with your thoughts. "Do not come too close," say the invisible signs which hang there. The walls themselves are invisible—so see-through that at times you are not even aware you have erected them. Of what are they made, these walls that keep others at bay? Of energy—like an electrified fence around a prison, and you are the prisoner.

Why hold yourself in solitary confinement? This is not your natural state. It is a state of fear which holds you there. What is fear, but the absence of love. It is quite a paradox, for often fear arises from the false thought that you will not get enough love. And so arise the walls.

You, my friend, have the Source of All Love within you. You are It. You are the love you seek. You need only be it, and reflect it, and radiate it outwards. This radiation is the most powerful force in the world. It has the power to knock down walls.

And so, as you send love outwards, you knock down the barriers that have been holding you apart from others, and in flows the love you have been seeking. Do you see how it works? Love ardently. Knock down your walls, and receive love in abundance in return.

May 12

THIS PATH YOU'RE ON

Bellows stoke the fire.
Air does fan the flames.
What began as just a spark
Now as a giant roar remains.

The path to your awakening
Is a bit like this.
There is no turning back, my friend,
Once you do taste the bliss.

You have that tiny spark right now.
It's waiting to be fanned
By thoughts and dreams and wishes,
And beliefs that once you banned.

So open up your mind and heart,
And fan the flames with glee.
This path you have embarked upon
Is the one that sets you free.

May 13

A TASTE OF HEAVEN

What is death, but a shift in your state of consciousness. In one state, you focus on the physical world, seeing through the eyes, interpreting all by how it looks, or feels, or sounds, and you think that these external things are the only reality. And then, in the blink of an eye, from one now-moment to the next, reality changes. You no longer have an eye to blink, fingers with which to feel, ears with which to hear, but lo! Behold! You are still alive! You must be, for you know that you are there. You are thinking thoughts. You feel the same. You know who you are, but everything around you has changed. Tune into this reality, and you realize that which you cannot feel with your senses you now feel so much stronger … you feel love, my friend, for you have come home.

Do not fear death. It is merely a transition. But do not hurry it along, either. You are here now to bring your true home to this experience. Love with all your heart and experience a taste of heaven wherever you go.

May 14

COMPASSION

Compassion … caring for another … feeling their pain and understanding how they feel. Compassion comes from knowing that at your core you are all the same. Even one who has no understanding of the truths of the Spirit can have compassion for another human, for the human experience is shared by all … birth, death, and the celebrations and trials in between.

It is the very presence of Spirit which gives rise to compassion. Human experiences will pass, but compassion remains, for its source is Love, and Love, like the Spirit, is eternal. See your brothers and sisters with compassion. Look upon them with love and honor the Spirit within all.

May 15

BE GUIDED

Haystacks … tall piles of straw … millions of pieces of matter that look alike, and somewhere buried in that haystack is a needle. How are you supposed to find it? When you have the right instruments, all tasks become simple. A very large magnet would make this task quite easy, would it not?

You have a beautiful divining rod there within you—a highly useful tool for sorting the wheat from the chaff. You call this your intuition. Like a magnet, your intuition can show you what you need attract to you and what you are best to repel. Like the needle, it appears hidden at times. It is only a matter of knowing it is there, this tool of the spirit. Listen to that gentle inner urging. Do not be like the millions of others marching to the same tune. Follow the voice inside; and like a magnetic compass that always points north, be guided unerringly.

May 16

COME OUT, COME OUT

Do not retreat into your cave when things do not go as you wish. There is a difference between going within and sitting in the silence, and going within a physical hiding place and sitting in solitariness.

It is far better when suffering to be with other souls. Do not wait for them to make you feel better, but radiate love outward, even if you can only muster a small glimmer.

Serve. Serve others, for in so doing you are connecting at the soul level, and this will bring about far more healing far more rapidly than sitting alone and licking your wounds. The latter only brings about more misery as you focus solely on the self.

Place your focus on others. Through these vital connections, you will experience humanity and realize that others suffer as well. Others rejoice as well. They are there to remind you that life is full of ups and downs and life does go on. So go on. Come out of your cave and live. In so doing, you allow your love to flow instead of stagnating. This flow brings vitality, and with renewed vitality you get back into the flow of life.

EGO VS. SPIRIT

Carry on, even when the road gets bumpy. You may wish to stop exposing yourself—always so vulnerable to attack—but it is the ego that says, "Look out. Be on guard. We do not want opposition." It is the spirit that says, "All is in perfect order. Fear not. Simply follow your heart."

It matters not what others think or say about you, for the "you" of whom they speak is not the spirit-being, but the human-being. Were they to speak of the spirit-being, they would be speaking of their very self, for there is but one spirit. It is the ego in others and in you which causes the human-being to judge. Allow yourself and others to be human, but always remember who you are—a spirit-being … pure love at the core. Let others say and think what they will. It is only blindness that does the judging.

May 18

SURRENDER

Surrender is not weakness. It is one of the most powerful actions you can take, when what you are surrendering is the ego. In this way you say, "I know that the ego is not my true self." The ego wants and needs to be in charge for its survival, but in giving full dominion to the false self, you do negate the presence and power of the spirit within.

With the utterance of two simple words, "I surrender," you do announce to the ego that there is a greater Force in charge. You do give up all need to control and let the Source of Love and Wisdom work through you. It becomes as a flow of energy and direction, directing your thoughts and actions instead of a willful "I know what's right" attitude. When Spirit is finally allowed to flow and direct, through the simple act of surrender, then miracles can and do occur. Surrender is not an act of weakness, my friend, for as you have heard, blessed are the meek.

FLY FREE

You are free … free to explore and discern—a free spirit, unencumbered by beliefs and misperceptions. It is the ego which does believe it needs to think and act a certain way. It is the ego which puffs itself up with names and titles and credits. The only reason one need join organizations is the fellowship, but never need you be told by another what to think or what to believe. Even these very words are but suggestions to open your mind to free thinking.

Succumb not to the group mentality. Always will there be those within groups in whom the ego dominates. Not always are they the most obvious—those who take the lead or beat the chest. Oft they are those who cling and appear the most needy, when in reality this is yet another of the ego's ploys. If there are those truly in need of succor, then give it, but fall not into ego's trap. Remain a free spirit. Discern truth and follow your heart. Give love freely, but give not your soul in support of the ego. You are free to fly, dream, and discover. This need not always be in a flock.

May 20

BE FEARLESS

Fear is a subtle killer. It kills your dreams and it kills your hopes. It comes in the form of thoughts which tell you that you are not good enough or that you will not meet the expectations of yourself or others. Fear is a by-product of the ego, for were you to stand only as the presence of love—which is your true nature as a spirit-being—you would have no fear. You would have only the knowledge that all there is is love.

Love yourself fully. In so doing, you allow your true Self to shine forth. If there is anything to be "killed," it is the ego's grasp on your self. The spirit cannot be killed, for it is eternal and all-powerful. Listen to your thoughts. Catch those that are fear-based and cast them out. Do not resist or resent them, for do they not teach you? Send them on their way with love … these fears you now recognize as falsehoods and limiters. You need hold onto them no longer. Be your true Self. Be fear-less, stand tall, and be an example to all.

May 21

A SIMPLE RECIPE

Do not underestimate the power of love. It is a healing force beyond anything in the material world. As the highest vibration—lo, the only vibration from which all arises—it can be used to move mountains, as you have been told by one who learned to use this power fully.

Harness the very highest vibrations of love and heal not just yourself, but your world. How do you do this? By setting aside judgment, by ceasing to criticize, and by allowing life to unfold without fear. Recognize ignorance when you encounter it, and look upon it with detached compassion.

All of these are the ingredients in the simple recipe for being the very presence of love. That is what you are. The main ingredient in a life of love always begins with love. Adjust the seasonings with varying degrees of patience and understanding, then share this feast liberally, for the masses are quite hungry. With this very basic staple in your bowl, no one need ever go without sustenance.

May 22

VISITORS IN THE NIGHT

Visitors in the night …
Are they real?
They seem so close
Their breath you can feel.

You reach out to touch them
And then they vanish
But their memory now
You cannot banish.

Treasure these moments
These elusive dreams
The ones you question,
"Was that what it seems?"

Yes, my friend,
'Twas a loved one's kiss—
A way to acknowledge
They know you do miss …

Their presence around you
Their touch and their voice.
They know that their absence
Was not made by choice.

And so they do touch you
At night in your sleep—
A time when your dreams
Take you ever so deep.

In this quieter state
Is the time they can reach you.
Your belief in their presence
Has a lesson to teach you …

The loved ones you miss
You will see once again.
But not just in your dreams,
A brief thought now and then.

They await your reunion
So fear not and feel blessed
For this life is eternal
With this knowledge now rest.

May 23

LET YOUR TEARS FLOW

Weeping willow trees … their branches hang limply. Why do they weep? It is as if all of the strength has gone out of their limbs. Do you not feel the same way at times? Crying can leave the physical body weak and limp, but it is a cleansing process. Is there not great beauty in a weeping willow?

Release the tension. Allow built-up emotions to flow from the body. Shake your limbs … allow the entire body to shake and clear all blockages from the system. As you cleanse in this way, watch as you do stand taller and stronger. Raise your head and soak up the sunlight. The rains always do end. The rain is necessary for growth, so let the water flow, and allow yourself to grow.

THE MIRROR OF LIFE

Upon reflection, you realize that you were wrong. Upon reflection, the hurt you caused another is shown to you. In another's eyes what do you see, but your reflection? Do you not see that all of you suffer the same pain, the same grief, the same emotions, and the same joy? There is but one spirit. All of you are but reflections of the one diamond sparkling with billions of facets. You look at another and feel their pain. When you cause pain to another, you suffer as well … upon reflection … for you have hurt yourself.

All is one. All of life is a mirror, reflecting its experiences back at those who gaze upon it until they realize that they are the mirror, themselves. Look into a mirror today. Gaze deeply into your eyes and see there the reflection of your eternal soul. If love does not gaze back at you, begin now to reflect upon the pain you are causing yourself by not loving yourself fully. Your actions mirror your thoughts and emotions. If your thoughts are not fully loving, clean your mirror until it reflects the full beauty of the real you.

May 25

BE A SEER

Fortune tellers gaze into a crystal ball and predict your future. How do they know any more than you? If they are legitimate seers, they can read your personal vibration. All is energy, and all is there for all to see when one learns to attune to the subtle energy of spirit. You need not visit a seer to know what your future holds, for you create it from moment to moment with your thoughts. You have your own crystal ball behind your physical eyes. Gaze inward. What do you see ahead? If you do not like the view, change it now in your thoughts, where all physical reality begins.

You are far more powerful than you have led yourself to believe. Believe in the creative power of thought. Thoughts are energy, and you direct them with your mind. Be a seer. Look into the future, fill it with love, and fill it with your dreams come true.

May 26

THIS PROVING GROUND

Do you know that you come here for a reason? This is a proving ground—a realm in which you arrive knowing that you are Spirit, but then do deliberately forget this. It seems strange, but do you not see the perfection? In order to remember what you have forgotten, you must interact with other souls—some who have awakened fully, and others who still slumber. You learn by trial and error. You are forged by the fire and polished by repeated rubbing … all of this removing layers of darkness that cover your true light.

Some of you are old souls, having had a go at this proving ground more than a time or two. You are the example. Others are newer souls … still learning and perhaps stumbling a bit along the way, but how else does a child learn to walk?

What is the greatest lesson of all that all who wear the human body seek to learn and to remember? That you come from love, to love you will return, and that by expressing love at every turn you awaken and become that which you seek.

May 27

PASSION AND PURPOSE

Each one has a purpose. It is up to the individual to discern what it is and why one has chosen this experience in human form. The purpose of man in general is to learn to love more fully … to express your true nature, which is love. It is quite easy to live life on purpose. All you need do is be the very presence of love.

But what of your gifts? Do you not have particular abilities and skills which bring you great joy? What is your passion? Why do you link the word "passion" with "love"? It is because when you are passionate about a thing, it is far easier to express and be love. So find your passion, and there you will find your purpose. Do you see the connection? Give your gifts to others. Share your passion liberally, and you will find fulfillment.

May 28

COMPETITION

Competition … is it a good thing? It is if it serves to bring out the best in the human form, and thereby reveal the greatness of that which impels the human form—pure Spirit. It is when competition serves only the ego, that those involved in the competition do lose the value of the experience. If used to beat the chest and to feel oneself separate, then competition helps not the spirit.

Remember always that each being is unique in its abilities, but none is any more special than another. May competition serve to show that all are special. Your Special Olympics do this on a grand scale, showing that what is important is not the competition, but the revelation of the true spirit of love.

May 29

CHANGE AND GROWTH

Be prepared for change, for change is coming. It is the Law of Life. Everything changes in perfect order. Life is about growth. Can you stop a plant from growing? Only by removing Life. You are the same as the plants and trees which arise from a seed and grow according to a perfect plan.

Understand us well—we speak not only of the physical growth of the body, but spiritual growth as well. You are here to help your soul to evolve. The body will grow and change all by itself, but, my friend, the soul will not do so without choices made.

Will your soul stagnate, or will it grow and blossom beautifully? Love is the light and water which feed the soul. Joy is the fertilizer. The body, at a certain point ceases to grow. It has a limit, but spirit is limitless. The soul evolves and grows with no limitations. Love fully, be joyful, spread love and joy, and grow.

May 30

TAKE CHARGE OF YOUR LIFE

Take charge of your life. No longer be the victim. No longer blame others outside of yourself for your actions and your choices. When you were a child, you depended on others to teach and guide you. No longer need this be so, save for the lessons others can teach you in being more loving. Now that you can think for yourself, look within for guidance. If the voice that speaks to you is loving and guides you to act in your best interest, send gratitude and heed it. If the voice you hear comes from a place of fear or negativity, that is not your true self.

Take charge of your life. How long must you continue to pay the price for past decisions and memories? There is only now. You are here to enjoy each now-moment, not to wallow in a past that has passed.

Enjoy now fully as the powerful spirit-being that you are … as the very presence of Love. The only victim then is any thought that is less than truthful about yourself as you dissolve it in the light of the real you.

May 31

ENJOY THE JOURNEY

Disillusionment follows revelation, for after there is great excitement, the pendulum does swing back to the other pole. This you know as the Law of Rhythm. Be not discouraged when excitement turns to doubt. The voices you hear are real. The knowledge you gain is useful. Continue your learning, but be not always seeking. Simply be that which you seek now, and enjoy the journey.

There will be ups and downs, revelation and disillusionment; but when all evens out, there in the middle of the pendulum's swing, you will find growth as well as peace. Continue asking for guidance within, and the answers will come, along with the revelation that all is in perfect order always.

June 1

IS ALL JUST SCIENCE?

You are far more than your brain. Yes, the brain is a tool. Yes, the two sides do give you different perceptions of reality, but you can perceive reality without a brain, which is what those who no longer are connected with a physical body do. Your scientists do believe the brain is the only perception mechanism, and this is not so. From whence comes the brain? All arises from Spirit. All matter is a product of consciousness, not the other way around. Make this distinction clear, and you will understand the One True Reality. All arises from Consciousness and all is Consciousness.

The brain provides two mechanisms for perceiving reality. Perceive with the left hemisphere and see things logically. Perceive with the right brain and have so-called spiritual experiences such as bliss. The latter is yours with or without a brain, for you are a spirit-being first and foremost, and bliss is your true nature.

Both sides of your brain work together to allow you to operate fully in the physical world. The left allows you to focus on your human side. The right exists to remind you that there is more to reality than pure logic. Set logic aside. Set the ego aside, and experience the peace and joy that are eternally yours, with or without a brain.

June 2

YOUR INNER VOICE

That voice you hear in your head is your own, but it is also the Voice of God. Have we not told you countless times that there is only One Mind? You seem surprised when after much effort in the form of prayer, meditation, and asking for guidance, suddenly a voice which seems far wiser than your own begins to speak to you. The Voice is gentle and so very loving.

And now we ask you, why are you surprised? Have you not been asking for enlightenment? You are having a conversation with God. You are hearing from your True Self. Why is this so hard to believe? All there is is Consciousness. All is One. Sit in the Silence. Ask to feel the Oneness. Attune to Higher Consciousness. Along the way you will meet guides and angels who may speak in funny accents, but keep going as high as you can go. What is the highest aspect of yourself? Who are you? You are the Most Worthy. You are here to know your Self.

Welcome to your awakening.

FEELINGS

"Get in touch with your feelings." What does this mean? How can you not know what you are feeling? It is quite simple ... those feelings that are at the so-called "negative" end of the spectrum are of such a low vibration that you will do whatever it takes to cover them with higher vibrations. You know the tricks. But remember: All is energy. Energy cannot be destroyed, merely transformed. So you do not destroy your pain by covering it up; you merely cover it up, allowing it to fester and cause dis-ease, aches, and yet more pain.

How, then, do you transform these lower vibrations? By exposing them to light. Bring them forth. Wallow in them for a while, and truly feel what they feel like. Talk about them with those who can empathize, then give validity in the form of love to these feelings. Now that you have validated them, you no longer need hold onto them. Now wallow in the higher vibrations of love for your full self—full of the full range of all vibrations, but in need of only being and expressing love.

June 4

ALWAYS LINKED

People who come in and out of your life—if only for a brief moment—are there for your growth ... for your soul's evolution. Some you may know a lifetime. Others you may fixate upon for a few years, or perhaps a shorter period, but oh, the changes they do bring about in that period! None are there by accident. Embrace their presence in your life, whether they bring you happiness or sorrow. All give you exactly what you needed to learn. Know that you do the same for them, and when you come to a parting of your ways, be it by mutual agreement or a solitary decision, let them go. This, too, is part of your learning.

When these souls have parted from your now-moments, look back upon your time together and celebrate it for the growth that has occurred. Dwell not in the past. Look around you now and see the relationships you currently enjoy. Celebrate these as well. These, too, will come and go, but once you share your energy with another, always will you be linked.

ALL IN THE MIND

Scattered showers … tiny cells of rain
That put a damper on your plans and cause you pain.
Why can naught but sunshine in your life remain?

Loosen your belt … cut us some slack.
There is nothing that you truly lack,
Yet a little dampness you do attack.

There is nothing you need do
For everything you need will come to you.
All is in perfect order, this is true.

Clouds and sun are part of life.
With struggle and pain your world is rife.
There seems to be no lack of strife.

Your freedom comes when you do find
That pain and strife lie in the mind
When to your thoughts you remain blind.

The sun will come when you do raise
Your thoughts up high and fix your gaze
Upon the light that will amaze.

No random light is this that shines,
But that which God defines …
The gold which every man in his life mines.

June 6

HILLS AND MOUNTAINS

There is no magic pill to take away your pain … no instant solution to your ills and problems. Why do you think you are here, but to build your character by surmounting your problems? If the road were always flat and straight, you would grow indolent and lazy … the body slack, the mind and will as well. But with hills and at times mountains to surmount, you do grow stronger as you climb and struggle. Have you not found that you use different muscles when climbing than when descending? And even in the descent, which seems far easier, there is growth.

Enjoy the challenges in your life. Embrace them. Your life would lose its luster were there no ups and downs. It is in the contrast that you do learn and grow. Dig in deep. Find there the strength that is yours.

June 7

FINE TUNING

"Make me your instrument," you pray. You ask this with the sincere desire to serve, and this is most laudable; but please realize that in order to be the perfect instrument, you must learn the art of surrender. The will is a wonderful gift from the Creator, but it does allow you to go off on your own tangents at times, does it not?

If you wish to be used by Spirit in service, this is a cooperative effort. Because you never have the big picture whilst you walk about in a human body, surrender is a necessary step. Does this mean that you become a puppet? Not at all. It means that you learn to attune to your inner guidance before acting. It means that you listen to and feel those subtle, loving urgings that tell you the best course of action. It is to these that you surrender.

You wish to be the perfect instrument? You are perfect already. It is merely a matter of a bit of fine tuning. The desire to fine tune your thoughts and actions is the perfect place to start.

June 8

ALL THERE IS …

Love is all there is. Love is all there is. Love is all there is. Your famous Beatles did sing these phrases, did they not? Is this but a trite phrase in overuse, or is this a spiritual truth? You live in a world with fear, hatred, and evil, so how can you believe that love is all there is? It seems a mockery of spirituality, making those who believe these words seem foolish and naïve. Fear not. You who adhere to this most basic of spiritual truths are wise beyond your years. You have discovered the gold at the bottom of the pan.

You call Spirit a force … an energy … but is it electro-magnetic energy? Is it gravity? Is it kinetic energy? You search for a name for this basic, elemental energy that is Spirit, and we tell you now, you need not look for another name. This most basic energy is love. All is Spirit. All is therefore love. Love rules the universe, or there would not be a universe at all. Quite simple, is it not? Love organizes the universe, or there would be chaos. Love causes those who eschew violence, hatred, and evil to send yet more love in the direction of these baser vibrations and pull them higher, seeking balance.

There is only love, expressing itself in all ways, always. Love is all there is. Be that which you are, and there find peace. Seek love no more. Be love and be joyful. Love is all there is. Worth singing about, wouldn't you say?

June 9

THE SEAT OF THE SOUL

Straight to the heart, a jolt flows, making you start. Why this connection between your heart and others, when the heart is just a pump—a physical organ? Because, my friend, it is not the physical heart that jumps. It is the heart of the soul, which just happens to have its greatest concentration of energy centered upon the locus of the physical heart.

Scribes and poets have known this for eons, and thus the heart-organ did become the poetic symbol for love, for who can deny the feelings of love in the chest when one cares deeply for another? This is not the physical organ where the feeling resides, but the heart chakra, as you do call it. Tune in to this vibrant energy center and feel the love. Sit in the silence and ask to be filled with love. Focus on the heart center and experience your true nature.

June 10

AT YOUR BECK AND CALL

"Gather your wits about you."
What exactly does this mean?
To make sense of what you see
And the spaces in between.

You do never know as much
As the mind will make you think.
And so for far more wisdom
From Spirit's font do you now drink.

Feel not so bounded by your self,
For bounded you are not.
The source of all you seek outside,
Inside you have you got.

While man can see about as far
As the horizon there before him,
There are spirit guides who wait to help.
They never do ignore him.

You have this source of help here now.
It's at your beck and call
Awaiting just to lift you up
If you should ever fall.

So gather, yes, your wits right now
And ask for guidance true,
For you are linked eternally
With guides who work with you.

IF … THEN

There is no "If … then" with God. There is nothing you need do or promise in order to get what you need. You need not bargain with your Maker. Do you not realize that you are one with God? You are the One Eternal Mind expressing Itself in this particular lifetime as a mind with a given name.

There is no need to bargain with your Self. The only need is to realize who you are and how Mind works. *If* you reach this beautiful point of realization, *then* you will co-create what you need. *If* you act and think as the God-being that you are, *then* you will begin to see miracles in your life.

June 12

CLIMBING OUT OF THE RUT

What happens when you get in a rut? You try to dig yourself out. You spin your wheels, getting no traction, and you just dig in deeper. You get discouraged and give up, and there you do remain, falling deeper and deeper into despair. You need a lift out. How to find it? By doing something new.

Change your habits. Change your outlook. Change your focus. All of life is about change. The rut comes in the first place when you do stay in the same place by habit instead of seeking change deliberately.

Are your prayers always the same? Your goals and aspirations? Where is your focus? Is it always on yourself or the same few people? Try a change in any aspect of your life. By moving your wheels in a different direction from time to time, you do not allow a rut to form. By taking on a new focus—most especially one outside your current deep rut and outside of yourself—you do raise your spirits, allowing you to depart the rut on your own. Never forget: You are the master of your own destiny.

A NEW OUTLOOK

Do you feel trapped in your circumstances? You can always run away. "Oh, I could not do that!" you say, for you are aware of circumstances. This shows you have a heart. You do not wish to hurt others by taking selfish action. You also fear change. These thoughts and emotions hold you in place to continue the situation. But, Beloved, it is your thoughts and emotions which do also set you free.

Have you become trapped in your mind … a prisoner of your thoughts? How else might you view your current situation? Might outsiders view it differently? Might outsiders view you differently? Might Spirit view all differently—in a more positive light?

Step outside of yourself. Step outside of your situation, and from this higher perspective, what can you see? What can you learn? What opportunities lie here besides running away or letting your thoughts run away and make you miserable? From this higher perspective, create a new outlook. Devise some changes. See your situation not as a trap or a prison, but as an opportunity. Now step into the future. Look back, and see how you have grown. See how you have been the expression of Love. And all of this you do with God's blessing, for you are never alone.

June 14

GO WITH THE FLOW

Change comes slowly for some and like a speeding train for others, but always it arrives. All of life is about the process of change. Those who accept this and adapt do thrive. Those who fight it and dig in their heels do suffer. There is only one thing that is changeless and eternal, and that is Spirit. It is Spirit which pervades all things, suffuses all things, guides all things, *is* all things. All is Spirit. All is a manifestation of Spirit ... Spirit expressing itself—the one constant.

Go with the flow. Accept change as the expression of Spirit. You are Spirit manifesting and expressing. How will you express your true nature? By digging in your heels, or by rising up and accepting the challenges in your life as part of Life itself? Life is far more enjoyable when you attune to Spirit and flow with it.

CRAWL UNDER THE BLANKETS

You can practice awareness and loving-kindness every moment, making every moment of your existence sacred. Be ever mindful of your thoughts. Are they as high as they can be, or do they drag you down? Are you seeing your brothers and sisters with compassion and empathy, or as separate beings with no connection? Go within, to that point of unity. Spend time there on a regular basis, and you cannot help but feel your oneness with all that is.

This is why it is so very important to meditate. When you walk only in the consciousness of a mortal being, you lose touch with that side of yourself which is eternal. It never goes away, but becomes as if covered by a blanket. Crawl under the blankets, dear child, and there find the warmth and comfort of love. Do not stay out in the cold and long for this state of warmth which is your birthright. Walk about at all times draped in the mantle of love.

June 16

CHARACTER BUILDING

What are you to make of talk of aliens and extraterrestrials? It is very simple. Study the concepts if you find them interesting. Why study genealogy? Why study history? Why study astrology and astronomy? You do all of this to broaden your knowledge and understanding. If any of it is true or false, what difference does it make in your character?

Aha! Do you see? This is what you study and work upon in parallel with all of these other topics of interest: character building. Where do you find information on that? Yes, from books. Yes, from others who lead by example, both good and bad, but also you find it in the heart—the seat of the soul. It is this very soul that you exist to develop.

Your character does not grow by understanding if you were once an extraterrestrial or a princess. It grows by your thoughts and actions here and now. So, explore other realms in your mind, in your books, and on your Internet if you wish. Enjoy your explorations, but in every moment explore how you can raise your consciousness, and hence your character, to the highest possible level. This is why you exist.

June 17

LOVE AND LIGHT

All colors become one in white light. Why do you speak of love and light together? Love is all there is, and all of the colors you perceive are held within the light. You speak of the "spark of the Divine" within you as light, and it is the perfect analogy. You exist to recognize yourself as the Light and to shine as brightly as possible—in love and light.

Even your scientists recognize the "allness" of light. It behaves as both a particle and a wave—it is the sum total of all potentiality. All possibilities are held within the Light. And so, beloved one, all possibilities are held within you. Sit in the silence and behold the Love and Light within. Behold the possibilities, and then awaken, and let your light shine.

June 18

YOUR ROLE IN THE DRAMA OF LIFE

How many roles do you play? Count them some time. You may be surprised. Do you consider yourself a mother or father? A daughter or son? A boss, a teacher, a retired person of leisure? A caretaker? These roles you play do change from day to day and moment by moment. You shift costumes so easily, playing some roles better than others. In fact, award-winning performances do you give in some cases.

The problems begin when you take these roles too seriously and they consume your life. Do you not see that all roles in the drama "Human Being" are temporary? You step on and off the stage, playing each role, but suffer when you begin to think that a particular role is who you really are. Beware. Even those roles in which you help others can cause you suffering if you believe that that particular role is who you really are.

Who are you, really? Take away all of the roles, and there you will find the Real You. At any moment you can be the director. At any moment you can sit in the audience and watch yourself playing your roles. Do not get caught up in any role. None of them is more important than another, save whatever role you are play-acting in this very now-moment. Are you playing it to the best of your ability? Will you win the prize for your expression of loving-kindness? As the director of this focus of your eternal existence, that is what matters most.

SWEET AND SOUR

Pickles … a strange word to hear in your meditation … but what are they? Fine vegetables mixed with a bit of vinegar, or perhaps a bit of sugar, to create a pungent taste which some enjoy. All beings have different tastes. Some like sour, some sweet. These you derive from adding ingredients to the mix.

Your life is like this – a basic good ingredient to which you add flavorings. Some days are sweet, others sour. Some events are to your liking, others not, yet do you not revel in the variety? Know that whether or not your day is sweet or sour, beneath it all lies basic goodness. In the case of life, that goodness is Spirit, and Spirit is Love. It is you who adds the flavorings. May they be to your liking, and if not, know that you always have the choice to change them.

You do laugh at our choice of analogy today,
But we dare say,
You will never again view
A pickle in the same way.

June 20

TIMELESS

Forever is a long time in your limited thinking, but forever has nothing to do with time. It is time which has limits. It is Spirit which is limitless. Spirit exists everywhere at once. In such a state, there is no time or place. Spirit simply *is*, and you are Spirit. So why do you perceive a world of time? It is an artifice, allowing you to experience each now-moment in succession in order to learn from them.

In the world of pure spirit, we pick and choose our now-moments. You in human form must watch them unfold from A to Z. In the spirit world, we choose to experience N or O or W, or perhaps Z to A, or perhaps the entire alphabet at once, for the entire alphabet which we use now as an example already exists. All exists, for all is Spirit.

Forever is not a long time at all, when time is only an illusion. You exist. It is as simple as that.

June 21

WHERE IT ALL BEGINS

Climb to the top of the highest mountain. There shout into the air your greatest desire. Do you think it will be heard better from these heights? My friend, we wish to tell you that your greatest desires can be whispered under the covers in your bed where no one will hear them, and they will be heard. Do you understand the difference?

There is physical hearing, and there is hearing without words. Your every thought is "heard." Your every desire is felt, for these are created in the mind and heard by the Infinite Loving Mind. They cannot help but be heard, for your mind is intimately linked with the One Divine Mind. How could it be otherwise, if there is only One? You are within the One.

So climb the mountain, if you wish. This may help you to see into eternity, but once again, you are using the physical eyes. Use the eyes of Spirit which are yours forever. Look inside and see there eternity. This is where you create your dreams. This is where it all begins. If you are unhappy with any element of your life, you need not climb mountains. You need only realize who and what you are.

June 22

SWEETNESS

Applesauce is the food of the day, in our continuing discussion of goodness. Why do you take perfectly good apples and turn them into mush? Because, in crushing them, you do release the sweetness. Some would not partake of this sweetness if the apple remained hard and firm. And so, you do make the apple easier to swallow by reducing it to a mushy consistency. Do you notice the necessary step to making it easier? Yes, first you had to take something that was hard and break it down.

Are not your greatest lessons like this? Do you not feel strong at times—perfectly solid, with your feet on the ground? And then along comes an event which crushes you and reduces you to mush. At first you feel as if your life has been destroyed, but after a while—at times a long while—you are able to look back and see how you have grown … how you have changed for the better. In this growth lies the sweetness of life, and in this understanding your difficulties are now easier to digest.

You do feed applesauce to your babies, for they cannot yet handle the harder foods. As you evolve, you are able to handle the challenges better and better. And always, when you can look upon your challenges from the greater perspective, they are easier to digest, and you will find the sweetness.

June 23

FLAVORINGS

Celery sticks … perhaps you do not like them, for to you they taste bland. Yet others do enjoy their texture and flavor. Why do you use celery in your soups and stews, but for flavoring? A useful dietary tool is this celery, for it is healthy, yet adds few calories to your intake. Why are the tasty things fattening and the bland celery not so? Are you not attracted by the very things that you should stay away from? Life lessons, once again.

Always you have a choice of what to enjoy, but what is enjoyed is not universal, for all have different lessons to learn. Some do not enjoy chocolate. (Can you imagine?) It is this variety that is the spice of life. It is for this reason that you add celery to your soup—for variety. It is for this reason that celery and chocolate and the billions of manifestations of matter occur—for the expression and experience of Spirit. As an expression of Spirit, yourself, you do always have a choice of what to eat, what to enjoy, what to eschew, and how to react to all things and events.

How wonderful is this gift of life! How very varied! Look around you today and truly appreciate the variety … savor the flavor of Life.

June 24

I AM

I am the bird that sings
And I am the song,
And I will continue to sing
All day and night long.

For I am forever.
I go not away.
Like the sun that does rise
At the dawn of each day.

I am not here to worship.
I do not want your desire.
I wish you only to know
That you can rise so much higher.

You and I are the same.
It is I who does breathe you.
And with this great knowing
Know that I'll never leave you.

So rise from your knees.
Pray to me if you must.
But it is only the body
That will return to the dust.

You are spirit right now.
You are me in expression.
It is your task in this lifetime
To learn this one lesson.

I am what makes the heart beat,
And I am the heartbeat.

I am what makes you breathe,
And I am the breath.

I am what makes the bird sing,
And I am the song.

I am what awakes you each morning,
And I am awakening.

I AM.

I am in all things,
And all things are in me.

I am in you,
And in the stillness you will know …

I AM.

June 25

HOW MANY WAYS?

How many ways can you say, "I love you."? How many words can cross your lips? How many ways can you form your hands and arms into instruments of love, be they used for a caress, a hug, or to carry a heavy load? This body you've been given exists to express love. Yes, you can do this quite well through the sexual act, but how many other ways can you use the body to live your purpose? Be creative. Be imaginative.

Love is what you are at your core. Be like the volcano, and erupt with love. Let it flow and then overflow as you get more experienced at expressing your True Self to the point where others notice the eruption and begin to do the same, for love is contagious. How many ways can you show it?

June 26

LIFE IN FOCUS

Your experiences are always a matter of focus. What is focus, but a deliberate placing of consciousness. You are so very focused now in the reality known as "the physical world" that this is your principal experience. It is when you shift your focus to a world beyond, that you do open the doors to new experiences. This causes a shift in your consciousness, and lo! A new reality appears.

It is a bit difficult for some to make this shift, for the human focus is so very deeply rooted in the present reality, but with belief, intention, desire, and determination, it is possible to experience other realities at any time. Some of you have done this and do so on a regular basis. How is this possible at all? Quite simple, my friend, because *you* are a focus of Consciousness, yourself. When you align your desire with the desires of your True Self, then all comes very closely into focus.

June 27

LOVE IN ACTION

Have we not told you that you are never alone? And yet you walk about feeling lonely. You do turn your music up loud so as not to feel so alone. Why do you crave the presence of others? This is understandable, and not a cause for guilt. Life is about relationships and learning to love through interaction with others. But know that it is the time when no other humans are present when you learn to love yourself.

You cannot love others in a healthy, non-clinging manner until you realize that the Source of Love lies within. And this is why we tell you that you are never alone. You walk with Love, for Love is your Source. You are the expression of Love, temporarily in human form, but eternally Love in action, whether taking form or not.

Walk about today and be yourself. Whether alone or with others, be Love. Let it transform your actions. Acting in this way, you will not and cannot know loneliness.

June 28

ALONG THE PATH

You are never quite the same once you begin your spiritual journey. Once you open your mind to possibilities greater than yourself, these possibilities become reality. You discover there really is a God. You discover you are greater than you ever imagined. You discover you are connected at the level of Spirit with all that is. You discover that Spirit is all there is, and once you make this discovery, try as you might, you cannot go back to small thinking.

You may give up your meditative practice for a while. You may go back to focusing on material matters for a while. You may pull into your shell and focus on only your troubles for a while, but after a while dissatisfaction wells up, and you know within where relief lies. It lies back on the path … the path that leads to joy and peace. And so, the journey continues … never ending, but always satisfying, for the journey truly *is* the destination.

June 29

BEWARE

Hurricanes … storms of great strength and fury which wreak havoc on the physical world. Do you not name an alcoholic drink after the hurricane as well? This is a bit of a joke in your world, to name a thing after another, but can the drink not be just as destructive as the storm, in its own way?

What is a name? It is but a symbol you give to a thing, and quite often to something that is not even real, such as "the devil." A mere word or name can wreak havoc and bring real fear, whether it is real or not. The hurricane is a very real force which does wreak havoc, oft times with the mere mention of the word. And so, be impeccable with your word. Be alert to the words you use, as well as the words used against you. They are all naught but symbols until you give them meaning.

You create storms in your mind with thoughts that become words. Take control of your thoughts and choose your words carefully. Choose your reactions with equal care. All of this requires attention and awareness, lest you be tossed about unnecessarily by the storm. "Beware" means nothing more than "be aware."

You create your own reality. Be aware of that.

TRUST

What happens when you have a lack of trust? You do close yourself off from another. You shut down your radiations of love and loving thoughts. Know it or not, the other does sense this at the level of spirit. On a human level, this distrust is sensed through the intuition, and the other behaves in just the way you feared. Understand that if you open yourself and radiate waves of loving trust to the one you—in your ego mind—do not trust, you can turn a situation on its ear.

Try it today. Give one your full confidence. Allow another liberties you would not have henceforth given (within reason, of course, for you would not send a child into a busy street). Know that the recipient of your trust will feel this and respond positively. It is positively the Law of Attraction in action. You get what you expect. So, trust us. We expect nothing less from you.

July 1

SHUDDER TO THINK …

You shudder to think of what may go wrong, but that is because you are thinking of what may go wrong! That is where your focus lies, and your body does react in kind by shaking. Do you see how body-matter follows thought? You would not shudder at all if you did not consider awful things as possibilities or consider possibilities as awful things.

Take all possibilities back to neutral, and decide how you will interpret them. If you wish to shudder and to be frightened, then go ahead and place your focus on fear. Interpret situations real or imagined as frightful, but understand that all is perception. You can take the most frightful or awful event you can imagine. (And my, can you not do a wonderful job at this?). Imagine it now from the perspective of higher consciousness, where you can see all as a great drama playing out. Sit back and watch, and when things get too frightful, shudder not, but change the scene. You do this in your mind with your interpretations.

Shudder to think what might happen if all human beings took control of their thoughts … then there would be no need to shudder at all.

NO NEED TO JUDGE

God does not dole out favors. God does not sit on a throne. Most importantly, God does not judge or condemn. God *is.* Spirit is the causative force of consciousness, and this Force is infinitely wise and infinitely loving. Were it not so, you would not even exist.

If God does not judge others, then why do you? It is because the lower, human aspect of yourself, which you do call "ego" needs to prove its existence. The ego proves its importance by showing its separation. By judging another, ego says, "Look at me! I am better than that one. I am superior." But Spirit does not judge. There is no need for Spirit to prove separation or superiority. Do you see how frivolous this would be? It would be as if saying, "I am superior to myself!"

There is naught but Spirit—Infinite Loving Consciousness—and you are an aspect of that. When you, at the level of Consciousness, finally grasp this most basic concept of Life, the need to judge disappears and is replaced with compassion for all. You may sit back and observe differences, but you do so always with compassion instead of judgment. This, beloved friends, is Love in action.

July 3

THE PART OF YOU THAT NEVER DIES

Fly away to worlds unknown.
This, my dear, is your true home.
You walk awhile upon the earth,
But in every moment you take birth.

You are born again each time you blink,
For Life is far more than you think.
Not just this time you walk as man.
That's just one blink in God's great plan.

You live, you breathe, you blink, you see.
You do it all eternally.
As God's expression, this life you live.
For now to God a form you give.

So use it well, this life you lead,
This one in which as man you bleed.
But know that underneath it all
You do not bleed, you cannot fall.

If all does seem a mystery,
Look not back upon your history,
But go within where Spirit lies—
The part of you that never dies.

July 4

PEACE IS THE GOAL

Peace is the goal … peace on earth and peace in your heart. Is this not where all peace begins: in the calm, stillness within? This stillness is always there, just as it is always still at the bottom of the pond, in spite of whatever waves ripple the surface. You are like the pond. Whilst you may experience turmoil all around you, the peace lies ever waiting within. Know that this is the part of you—your True Self—that is ever-present and ever-accessible.

Call not upon things or people external to yourself to bring you peace, but summon the peace that lies within you and bring it to the surface. Radiate tranquility and watch the waves around you subside. In this way, you can be a peace-maker, for yourself as well as for others.

Peace be with you … always.

July 5

A WEB OF YOUR OWN MAKING

'Tis far better to err than to never try at all. So many sit and dream of things beyond their reach, but fail to act for fear of failure. This is the ego thinking. You are caught in a web of your own making. The more you struggle in your mind, the more trapped you do become. Realize that you are the one who has sewn the web. You walk upon the gossamer strands. You create them yourself. You are not their prisoner.

Have you not seen a spider's web sparkle and glint in the light? Shine the light on your fears and see them for what they are: misperceptions and illusions of your own making. Nothing can hold you back from your dreams but the very web of your thoughts. Put the web behind you and strike out boldly in the direction of your dreams.

July 6

FIRESTARTER

You rub two sticks together and you create heat by exciting the molecules. Higher vibrations are creative. Raise the vibrations even higher and you create fire. Lo! You have created light! What if you had the ability to raise the vibrations ever and ever higher? What if there were no limit to the vibrations you could raise? Why, then, could you not create a universe?

It is all a matter of degree, my friend. You are consciousness in human form … for now. From Consciousness you have arisen. Call it what you like: Call it Consciousness, call it Spirit, call it God, call it the Creative Force of the Universe … you are *It.*

For now, you are a small focus of "It," but do you not have the ability in this moment to create fire and light … and yes, love? Call it Mind, call it Infinite, call it Infinite Loving Mind. If you are "It," and you are endowed with the same creative force as the Creator, then use it to create more love in your world. Why else would you be here?

Any man can build a fire, but once you see the light, how will you use it?

July 7

ON WINGS OF LOVE

Never fear the truth. We speak now not of truth in the sense of the human word, which can be twisted in endless ways to meet your means. We speak now of the truth that never changes …

Do not fear love, for love is what you are. This is the truth of which we speak. Seek love in all things, yes, but *be* love first and foremost. Judge not another for their lack of love. Judge only yourself, but not with criticism, with love, my friend. Do you see?

Fear nothing. Judge nothing. Be only love. This is your main task in life—your *raison d'être.* Be aware at all times of thought and feelings. These work in harmony, and when they truly operate in harmony, then the soul sings. Be a walking song of love, fearless in knowing the truth, fearless in your expression of the truth, and the truth truly will set you free to soar like eagles—to fly as the true spirit-being that you are on wings of love.

A WHOLE NEW WORLD

Do you want to see your world with wonder? Step outside of the box you have placed yourself in. Boxed in … that is what you are … boxed in by your conditioned thoughts and actions. You are Consciousness, constantly creating your reality with your thoughts, but like a mouse on a wheel, round and round you go once you get used to the motion. You forget or do not realize that there is a world of other motions available to you when you step off the wheel and climb out of the cage.

The ego likes its routines. Routines make you feel safe in your little box, but you are not here simply to be confined. You are here to create, to explore, to enjoy the wonder of creation and the wonder of being you. Look at the box you have created, then ask yourself, "In what new ways might I act, might I respond, might I dance today? Instead of going round and round on this treadmill, might I instead move side to side and there discover new joys?"

Step outside of the box into the world of pure potential. Dive into the sea of possibilities and explore a whole new world.

July 9

THE MUSIC OF LIFE

All arises from the silence. Think of your music. There would be no awareness of music at all, were it not for the spaces in between the notes. It is from the stillness—the perfect calm—that beauty is expressed. And so, a note is sounded, and then another, with enough of a difference in vibration that the mind detects variation. And then another note and yet another is sounded. In your system, you have a scale which you call an octave. Certain notes vibrate within this scale in resonance with others, and there is dissonance with some. Do you not see how all of life is represented in the sound of music? Variation of vibration along limitless octaves… resonance and dissonance, and all arising from and returning to the beautiful silence.

Why do you think some songs attract you like magnets? They pull you into their beauty in such a way that your heart soars when you hear the notes and the beautiful chords. Are not you attracted to some people in this way? To some scents? To some sights? All is One, my friend. All is the vibration of Love in expression, and all arises from the perfect stillness in order to experience life in its infinite forms. These are the infinite symphonies of life.

You—in your current human form—are but one note in one symphony at this moment, but life is eternal and ever-present. The song is ever-changing. You are the note. You are the song. And where do you draw the line between the note and the silence? You cannot, for one flows into the other. You cannot have a song without both. You are intimately intertwined with the music of the Maker.

YOUR DAY WILL COME

Every man will have his day. Do not wait for fame and fortune. These are things of the material world. Wait only for that golden moment when the Light fills you so completely that you feel as if you could burst … when you are so filled with love of life, of nature, of your fellow man, and yes, of God, that you raise your head and arms to the sky and shout, "This is why I am here! To have this day! To have this moment and every moment that follows!" And then, when you have had this moment—your "day"—you can handle the valleys and those days that seem mediocre. Yet, are not all of them helpful in making those bliss-filled moments all the more special?

Do not worry if your day has not yet come. Do not worry if it has passed. These days are all around you. They are Life in expression. Do not sit and wait, nor worry when they will come. Get out and live your life to the fullest. Love fully, with all your heart, and then, dear heart, your day cannot help but come.

July 11

ENEMIES AND LOVERS

Make your enemy your lover … a shocking statement, is it not? Why do you love some and not others? It is most often because some agree with you and others do not. Do not all humans have the will to choose their thoughts and actions? Allow them to do so. If all thought and acted the same, there would be no point whatsoever in having this life experience.

Treasure the differences in each other. Surely, it is obvious when some abuse free will and act in unloving ways. See this with compassion and understanding. Forgive those with whom you may have disagreed in the past over some triviality. Oh, we hear you now, beginning to argue: "But it was not trivial!" We disagree. All is trivial except loving thy brother as thyself. And so, see the disagreement for what it was and what it is: differing expressions of the Love Force … differing levels of understanding of the Truths of the Spirit. And then, make your enemy your lover.

What is a lover, but one you love without condition. Love fully, and there find peace. Love fully, and there find your reason for living.

FILLED WITH WONDER

Synchronicity … a word you hear much about when you are on the spiritual path, and one with which you have more and more experience the more you attune to Higher Consciousness. When two events come together in what to you seems a miraculous way, much like the perfectly timed movements of your synchronized swimmers, you call this a synchronicity. It is these moments that show you the perfection of life and allow you to see that there are greater forces at work than the smaller self.

These are eye-openers, meant to fill you with wonder so that you no longer wonder, "Is there a God? Do I have helpers? Am I alone?" No, my friend, you never walk alone, and synchronicity is a gift from this God who breathes you … a gift to fill you with joy and make you say, "Can you believe what just happened?" Yes, you can believe it. And that is the point. When you synchronize your will with the will of your Greater Self, synchronicities become the norm.

July 13

FAMILY MATTERS

Family is so very important. Why? Because you made an agreement before you came here to learn from each other and to help each other to evolve and grow. Some of you are very close in temperament, style, and appearance, whilst others seem as if they belong to a different clan.

Do you see the learning opportunities these differences offer you? "To learn what?" you ask. "To learn of pain and strife?" No, to learn to love each other no matter what. You can learn this with all those around you, to be sure—with friends, enemies, and distant strangers—but your family is ever-present, if not physically, then in your very genes. You may try to forget them, but they do not go away. This is because they will always have the very basic lessons of life to teach you. Thank them, and then get back to work on your lessons.

SAVOR THE SWEETNESS

Raspberries … such a beautiful fruit, bursting with sweet juice, and such a vibrant red color … so pleasing to the eye, yet what happens when you bite into the berry? There you find a multitude of seeds that become lodged between the teeth and prove irritating. And so, you find an alternate way of eating the raspberry. Instead of chewing, you press down lightly and thus enjoy the juice and the sweet flavor without the irritants.

Is not your life like this at times? Are there not numerous irritations and people who get stuck between your teeth, so to speak? They will always be there. They are part of the "berry," but are they not surrounded by sweetness and beauty?

Do not chew so hard. Do not bite down and grind away when the irritants make their presence known, but merely acknowledge they are there and savor the sweetness anyway. The seeds all play a role, as do you. Savor this life, irritants and all, remembering that irritants are in the mind. It is all in how you choose to consume each beautiful experience. Focus not on the seeds, but on the sweetness. It is all around you.

July 15

SOFTEN YOUR EDGES

Kittens have such soft fur that you could sit and stroke them all day. Why this attraction? The human body is beautifully attuned to that which resonates with the spirit. Inside, you are all goodness. It is only on the outside that some take on the rough edges. Are you prickly like a porcupine, or do you have the soft fur of a kitten? Others note this, but note that this is only a false exterior you have erected.

Inside, all is soft and furry. If you balk at this thought, you are referencing your ego side. The ego is built upon many falsehoods, not the least of which is that you are separate from your brethren. Take away the ego, and what do you have? A kitten with the power of the most gentle of lions.

Soften your edges and let the sound that comes from within be a gentle purr … a purr of satisfaction that comes from knowing that at your core you are Love.

HAVE A GOOD CRY

Why do you cry? You often hear it said that crying is a release, and this is so. Have we not told you that all is energy? Therefore, you have either a flow or a blockage. What do tears do, but flow? Tears are the conduit for blocked energy. Does not the body heave when wracked with sobs? This heaving is the same as when the body expels toxins from the stomach, only in the case of crying, all of your movements are directed at the expulsion of negative energy that has been stored and caused blockages. Why do you think it often feels good to cry? You are freeing blockages.

Perhaps you do not even know why you are crying. If you could read your tears as the carriers of energy which they are, there you would find the reasons … "Aha! There is my grief over loss." "Ah, so … there is my compassion for another's suffering." And, "Look! There is my perception of the way another treated me. Thank goodness I have released this energy."

And so you feel a bit "wiped out" after a good cleansing. This is a time of renewal. Treat yourself with loving care. The crying was a good thing. Is not the body the perfect instrument? Yes, at times it suffers from imperfections, but this self-cleansing mechanism you call crying is evidence of a good plan. Have a good cry now and then, and then get on with filling your body with love.

July 17

ISN'T THAT INTERESTING!

Failure is a human invention. As spirit, you cannot fail. As Spirit, there is only experience. How you choose to interpret each moment and each experience is up to you. If you, as spirit, gave credence to the illusory concept of failure, you would not choose to return to human existence. But you do choose, for you know that there exists naught in the human world but learning experiences.

See not your learning opportunities as success or failure. When you view your world in such a way, you do create much anxiety and low vibrations. You can instantly raise your consciousness by merely looking upon things that do not go as you hoped or expected and saying, "Isn't that interesting!" Then fill your heart with compassion for the human side of you which so bravely agreed to undertake this experience.

Yes, failure is an option for the human, but you are spirit first and foremost. As spirit—we repeat—you cannot fail. You are loved beyond words. Carry that thought in your heart and find the courage to soldier on in your human garb.

CHOICES

Bitter blows the wind, and you pull your coat tight about you. You shiver to keep warm. What is temperature, but an indication of the vibrations around you. You gauge these sensations and give them meaning. Some enjoy the heat, whilst others revel in the cold. Is not all of life like this: relative … full of comparisons … up and down, in and out, hot and cold, like and dislike?

Yours is a world of duality—of opposites which allow you to make choices and to take action based on those choices. Do you not see that this is how you grow? Rather than judging another for their perception of reality and for the choices they do make, focus only on yourself. Pull your cloak tight around you and go inside, where choices are made. There you will find no cold and hot, no up and down … only silence. From that silence arises all. When in a quandary as to what choice to make, always return to the silence, where all choices can be made from a place that knows only love.

July 19

BEYOND WORDS

You speak of "love beyond words," and why is it "beyond words"? It is so, because words are limited. Yes, there are only so many words that can express a thing that is not a thing at all—this thing you call "love." It is more than "love beyond words." It is "love beyond worlds." Love exists in all dimensions, in all forms, and without form. It is the basis of all being. It is your reason for being. You exist to express love in all forms for the very purpose of experiencing love beyond words.

The more you express love, the more you understand Reality. The reality is that love is the First Cause. Love is the only cause. There would be no you, there would be no world, were it not for love. In the beginning was the Word, and the Word was Love, and ever shall it be Love.

Go forth and share what you know in your heart. Be that which you are at your very core. Radiate it in every moment and your world will be changed forever. That is how Love works.

CONTRASTING COLORS

You see the differences in others. They think differently than you do, and of course this is so. The world is not black and white, but bursting with colors. Do not be frustrated that others think not as you do, but sit back and gaze at the variety as if viewing a masterpiece, for that is what your world represents.

How dull would be a painting, were it one solid color. How very interesting are those paintings with just the right mix of hues. Do you not see that it is the contrast that brings you pleasure when you view a painting? Focus not on one area of the painting, but see it all from a distance, and there you will see the brilliance.

Your world is full of minds, all stemming from the brush of the one Great Artist. There will always be minds apart from yours—at times miles apart. Do not let this disturb your own expression of the Artist. Stand for your own color, if you will, knowing that each color holds equal value in the Artist's eye.

July 21

SHIFT YOUR GAZE

Search in the clouds or upon the ground . . .
What you seek seems ne'er to be found.
Perhaps you've set your sights too high,
On what some would consider "pie in the sky."

You seek euphoria—a strong sense of peace.
From all your troubles you seek release.
Look all around you and what do you see?
That others wish also to be set free.

This bondage you feel is the human way—
"Trapped in your skin" at the end of the day.
But this is not true; you are free to fly
When you see the world with your inner eye.

True peace awaits when you close your lids
And do as the spirit inside of you bids.
Remove your gaze from the world outside
And place it where the heart does reside.

It's there true peace and love you'll find,
For these fine gifts lie inside of your mind.
And mind is eternal, as is the Real You.
Just close your eyes to find this is true.

July 22

RITUALS

Be true to your *self*. Try new things. Experiment with rituals you have learned of. Join a group that looks interesting. Sit in new positions. All of these things and more you can do in an effort to be more spiritual, but what does this mean, "to be spiritual"? Does it mean that you sit in a church every Sunday and sing? Does it mean that you sit cross-legged each morning and chant a mantra? Does it mean that you repeat the same prayer 100 times in a row? You can do all of these things or none of these things and still be spiritual.

If a certain action or tool brings you to a place where you are more centered, focused within, and more aware of your connection with God, then by all means, carry on. If, however, your rituals, ceremonies, and actions are done only out of fear that should you not do them some ill will befall you, then you have missed the point.

Try new things as you like, but pause every now and then and ask yourself, "Does this bring me into closer communion with My Source?" That, in the end, is all that matters, for that, in the beginning, in the middle, and in the end is why you are here.

July 23

WITH EVERY BREATH

With every breath you take, you grow more relaxed. With every breath you take, you sink deeper into yourself. With every breath you take, you return to innocence. With every breath, you shed the ego and become aligned more closely with The Source.

Take a breath and follow it. Where does it go? It goes into your center, from which all things arise. Allow the breath to settle there a moment, and simply be with it. Now follow the breath as you send it on its way, and then repeat this cycle of creation, existence, and dissolution. The breath may fade away, but always it is followed by another, as long as you continue to create your breaths.

"Yes," you think, "but what happens when the body ceases to breathe?" Then, beloved child of God, you no longer need oxygen, for God breathes you into a new dimension of life. With every breath God takes, you continue to exist. Whether here in a body that breathes, or after this physical life is extinguished, you continue as the breath of God. Breathe in deeply for now, and with every breath you take, know yourself as All That Is.

July 24

ALL ABOUT THE JOURNEY

Dinosaurs roamed your earth millions of years ago. They did come and go as species were changed and perfected. Theirs was a very turbulent world, with fighting among each other and violent earth changes. Much has changed in the interim, but in some cases, things have not changed. Now your earth is populated with Homo sapiens, and do you not see fighting among each other? Do you not continue to see earth changes?

Do not be frightened or overly dismayed by either. Fear and dismay only add to the lower vibrations of your earth. Look, instead, at the progress that has been made. You want change immediately, do you not? Yet, look at how far evolution has come, and how long in your time it has taken. For us, in the realm of no-time, it is the blink of an eye. We can see the big picture and are well pleased with the progress.

It is your focus on the destination of total peace and no disturbances that causes you frustration. Do you not see that a part of you already exists in this perfect place from which you arose? It is your rightful home. For now, you are taking a side trip in a world that is slowly evolving. You, by emanating vibrations of love, can help in this evolution. Do not dismay. Be part of the solution by radiating peace and fearlessness, knowing it is all about the journey.

July 25

CURRENTS

Undercurrents ... a lesser vibration you do feel in the midst of interaction with another. What is it that is not being said? You need not hear the words aloud, for you can feel the energy of thought. Energy flows in waves, and these undercurrents of lesser vibrations do disturb a relationship, for they reveal that full truth is not present. Were you and the other fully aware of the spirit, you could hide nothing from each other, but yours is a world of secrets.

Why do you hide the truth? You fear the other's judgment, disapproval, or anger ... all of which lead to a withholding of love, whether real or perceived. The only way to overcome this is with love. Send out your own greater wave of higher vibrations and wash away the undercurrent. Be truthful with yourself and the other, but always with a strong foundation of love, and there can be no room for lesser vibrations.

Do not waste a moment of life being anything less than you are—the very ocean itself.

FARMERS

Sowing seeds … that is what you are doing each time you share the truths of the Spirit with another. You plant an idea in the consciousness, and from there it sprouts and grows. Not all beings are ready to support such growth. Their belief systems have caused their ground to dry up, but others have fertile soil just right to promote growth.

Do you see how you can spread love throughout your world simply by sharing what you know to be true? Of course you must be cautious and selective. We do not wish to encourage any soul to push their beliefs on another. Use your sixth sense. When you cross paths with another who is suffering, do not unload the bulk of your wisdom at once. These are seeds we are speaking of. Dole them out like pearls. "Do you know," you might say, "that you can see this situation in another way?" And from there begin a discussion about compassion.

An example we give you, but you have the best advisor you could ask for inside you at all times. When sowing seeds, speak as the spirit-being, not from the ego, and you will be planting just the right crop.

July 27

BEYOND BLISS

What is ecstasy? It is a state of consciousness in which lesser vibrations are blocked to such an extent, that all you feel is love. The body reacts with joy, sending a rush of good feelings to all parts. The mind grasps at the flood of positive images. The heart threatens to burst. All of these reactions are naught but recognition, as if meeting a long-lost friend. "I have been searching for you!" the spirit cries. "And there you are! This is why I have felt so dissatisfied."

The spirit knows the heights to which it can soar. It longs to fly at all times, but the more dense vibrations of the physical world hold it back for a while. It is the gift of these moments of ecstasy which give you the strength to carry on. This feeling-beyond-words is your birthright, yet hear us well: It is only a scratch on the surface of the True Self. Could you but touch the face of the Self at will, you could not handle such bliss. And so, we give you a taste for now. This is ecstasy.

July 28

THIS PRECIOUS SEED

There lies within you a treasure so great, yet how often you ignore it. This treasure is like a seed that needs your tending. If you do not recognize it and give it light, water, and fertilizer, it will lie there as all seeds do, full of potential, but unrealized. This seed is the Christ of all beings. Do not let belief systems block you from appreciating the meaning of this word or the value of this gift. We speak now of that aspect of yourself which is Godlike. Not only was the one you know as Jesus the Christ child. All humans have within them the potential to be a Christ—a child of God.

You are this now. This seed lies within you, but as we said, it does need light, water, and fertilizer to be awakened. Your recognition of this potential within yourself is all that is needed to begin the process. That is the light. Your desire for this seed to awaken is the water. Your focus on growing this seed into a fully-realized child of God is the fertilizer. Tend to your garden, my child, and grow into the God-being that you are.

July 29

MILESTONES

You speak of your birthdays and anniversaries and make certain dates into special occasions. It is the importance you place upon these days that does make them important. Some birthdays and some recurring anniversaries you make even more important than others, such as those which coincide with your numbering system of fives and tens. This is a system of using time which can bring you joy, but also unnecessary pain, if you do dwell upon what to you are painful events recalled year after year.

An event is an event, nothing more than an opportunity to learn. Once passed, it is past. Do not dwell on these events which brought you pain, if only to dig up painful emotions. Live in this now-moment. If there were no time in your world, there would be no birthdays or anniversaries to celebrate or mourn. You would live as the spirit-being you are and simply celebrate each moment for your existence, and for the opportunity to be loved and give love.

Happy anniversary of this moment of Life.

THE PERFECT VEHICLE

Who is to say what is perfection and what is a handicap? Some blame God when there is born a baby that is not "perfect." This is because you are making comparisons with a pattern … with a norm. In your world of duality, you judge all along a spectrum, labeling it good or bad, when at its essence all simply "is."

The spirit is neither good nor bad. It simply is. It exists to express love. All matter is merely a vehicle for the experience and expression of love. If a body does not match the norm, is it any less of a vehicle for expressing love? Can it not be an even greater vehicle for doing so and bringing out the highest expression of kindness and compassion in others?

Look not upon an "imperfect" body with pity, but with love. See the perfect spirit-being inside which has chosen this vehicle as a way to provide a varied form from the norm in order that all may grow in love.

July 31

THY WILL BE DONE

Every breath you take is by the will of God. Every thought you have is by the will of God. You are co-creators. Nothing you do is a solitary action. Yes, you do have so-called "free" will, but even this is by the will of God. If your Creator did not wish for you to take a certain action or have a certain thought, that thought or action would be impeded like a parent reaching out and gently steering the child in another direction … no matter how will-full the child.

You think that when you exert your will that you do so solely. This is a misperception, for naught occurs without the assistance of God. Imagine how very easily all would flow in your life if you lived by the mantra, "Thy will be done." Then, my child, you would be in perfect harmony with All That Is. Be not as the rebellious child, but a full-fledged partner with your Highest Self.

August 1

THIS BLESSED GIFT

Yours is a world of infinite possibilities, bursting with potential. Do you feel despair? Are you discouraged? If so, you have shut yourself off from realizing the Truth—that all the world is yours. Your dreams can come true. We speak now not of the fancy car or larger home, but your dreams of finding peace, joy, and love. Of these elements there is no shortage—not in your world, nor any other.

Open your mind, but most especially your heart, to the Truth that you are deserving of all the love the world has to bestow upon you. You are the most worthy being in the Universe, as are all of your brothers and sisters. No one is spared this gift, but one must be open to receive it. How do you open to love? Again we repeat: by knowing you are worthy of receiving it. It comes not from others, but from your Higher Self, which is eternally yours. Ask and ye shall receive this most blessed gift that is waiting to be bestowed upon you.

August 2

LIKE A RIVER

Peace like a river … a very apt phrase for describing the way the vibration of love does flow through you. Why do you say that you feel warm in your heart when love is present? Understand that love is always present, but when allowed to flow freely, the higher energy of this highest of vibrations produces an actual heat. A healer's hands become hot from this healing energy of love, do they not? And always it does flow—yes—like a river, stopped only by the thoughts which dam it.

Staunch not this vital flow, but seek out the blockages so that the warmth fills not only the heart, but all of your being. There you will find true peace, in the depths of the river of love.

August 3

IN PERFECT ORDER

The entire Universe exists for your enjoyment. You are here to play and create, for who are you but a focus of the consciousness of the Great Creator. It is through your experiences that God experiences God's creations. How else would God be able to play?

Go forth each day with an attitude of playfulness and joy, knowing that all is in perfect order always. Let this be a mantra which falls from your lips at every moment. As you see things you question, for you think they are mistaken or wrong, say this important phrase again: "All is in perfect order always." As this phrase becomes part of your creative consciousness, sit back and watch the perfection unfold. Laugh with joy as you see what happens when you go through your day in harmony with the flow of the Universe.

A small coincidence is no longer "luck," but a living example that you are in the flow … part of Creation itself, helping to create the perfection that is Life. And then go out and play some more, creating yet more perfection. And as you do so, smile … for would not God smile down on God's creation and say … "It is good."?

August 4

BE INSPIRED

You are complete as you are. You need not search outside yourself for fulfillment, for you are Fulfillment, itself. Those who spend a lifetime seeking know not that which they seek, and thus do not realize that that which drives them to seek is the very part of themselves which they have not yet fully recognized.

Seek not outside yourself, but look inside. The longing which all feel for "something else" is the longing to be loved. Know that it is Love that created you and Love that sustains you in existence. Without Love you would not even breathe. But do you not see that you breathe because love flows through every cell of your body as you do so?

Breathe in the breath of Love, and exhale just as strongly. Be in-spired by Love, but know that Love does not expire. It lives forever, as do you. Be the Love that you are, and seek no longer.

August 5

YOUR CORNER OF THE STAGE

Patience is a virtue ... yet another of your pithy sayings, but one with great wisdom, for so many of you do rush about expecting to see results in whatever the endeavor, in accordance with your earthly timetables. But you do not realize that your earth is not the only dimension in which you play. While you are far from mere puppets on strings, you do all have unseen helpers from the unseen realm. In a way, we are pulling some strings for you, but it is always you who choose your reality through your choices.

On your earth you see the results of some of your choices instantly, whilst others take some time to manifest. In addition, you are all co-creators of your reality, and so there will always be outside influences, other causes, affecting your desired outcomes. But always remember: All is One. There is only one Divine Mind directing this great play of your life. You are bit actors—and we do say this most lovingly—but each with a most vital role: to be the representative of Love on your small corner of the stage.

You are the director of your part, and of your scene, but you have not yet seen the ending. Be patient. Awards will be given out at the end for he who plays the most loving role ... not for he who gets there first.

August 6

YOUR PERSONAL BAROMETER

Emotions … the perfect gauge of what is going on inside your head. Like a barometer, the pressure goes up and down, as does your personal vibration with every thought that passes through your mind. Your emotions are always the result of a thought, thus you control your emotions, for you always control your thoughts.

Do you wish to find more peace in your life? Then choose your thoughts carefully. Peaceful thoughts engender peace in mind and body.

Use your body as your personal barometer. Is the pressure high? Follow the sensation back to the source … the thought which caused your emotions to spike. Is the pressure low, leaving you calm and at peace? See how the choice of thoughts you made—not the actions of another—but the choice of thought you made, did result in your current state.

Your body is an instrument … a perfect gauge of your internal state. Use it to your benefit. When life is stormy, send calming thoughts. Look not outside and blame the wind, but go inside and be the cause of your calm. It is always a choice.

PERFECTLY IN TUNE

There is so much discord in your world … disharmony ... notes out of tune. "Out of tune with what?" you might ask. With the vibration that is always perfectly in tune … the vibration of love.

Picture your world as the notes on a scale, with many octaves. Love would be at the top of the scale … the purest note you could sound, yet attainable by all. The discordant tones are those which fail to resonate with the highest vibration.

Sing loudly as you go through your day. If you hear yourself singing a bit off pitch, you need only adjust your tune. Your mind is your tuning fork, and you attune to the highest vibration with your thoughts.

Like the opera singer, raise your voice … sing high and clear and perfectly in tune with the vibration of love … a sound of pure beauty that resonates in the heart of All That Is.

August 8

SHAPE YOUR THOUGHTS

Into every life there comes pain. This you have come to expect. You run from this pain, but do you not see that these times of trouble and suffering have produced the greatest growth in the quickest time? It is not that we wish you to suffer, merely to see the suffering for what it is—a tool of your soul's evolution. You have chosen your circumstances and the teachers in your life for a purpose. Welcome them for the lessons they bring you.

At the same time, know that all suffering begins in the mind. All events are neutral. The suffering comes from how you choose to interpret each event. True growth will reveal that you can control outcomes just as easily as you control your thoughts. The more you change your reactions to events which in the past may have created angst, the more you realize how very much you are created in the Father's image.

The Father creates only goodness. It is through man's use of this same creative Force—the power of the mind and will—that man creates darkness or light, suffering or peace. You are the creator of your personal universe. How will you shape it? Your thoughts are the clay.

August 9

NURTURE YOUR SPIRIT

Your Earth is a place of such beauty. The mountains that rise toward the skies call to you with their majesty. You have water in abundance, from small ponds to your greatest oceans, also calling you with their serenity. Yet cannot the oceans be as a tempest, changing character in mere minutes?

The natural things you see around you are but a reflection of the human soul … changeable, majestic, peaceful at times, stormy at others, but beautiful in their very nature. You now realize the importance of preserving your natural environment—these treasures which require care and safekeeping—but do you not realize that the soul requires tending as well?

Nurture your spirit. Treat all souls with loving care and watch how they grow and flourish. Love is the fertilizer. Spread it freely and reap the harvest.

August 10

MOVE THE STONE

So many of you carry a weight in your heart much like a stone. This weight blocks you from feeling and giving love, like a dam that prevents the natural flow. This stone is the rock of resentment toward another, held in place by the inability to forgive an act which you, with your limited vision, did perceive as wrong. Forgiveness is the force which frees the stone and allows the love to once again flow freely.

Whom does it serve to hold onto resentment? Neither you, nor the other. Yet whom does it serve to forgive? The answer is clear. Forgive, not to feel righteous, but to allow your True Nature to shine. It is the other who will pay in the end for their misuse of their personal power. You, yourself, need not pay.

All of you walk a solitary path of learning and growing. It is not yours to judge how another walks, for you walk not in his shoes. Walk your path with head held high and love in your heart for all others. Then you will have the power not just to move the stone from your heart, but the power to move mountains.

August 11

THE CALM SURFACE

See the ripples upon the water … a disturbance caused by some object which has touched the surface. But look below, into the very depths of the water, and you will find calm. Your mind is like the water of a deep pond. Always your thoughts do cause ripples upon the surface. At times these ripples may even become so perturbed as to have tiny whitecaps.

When so disturbed, you cannot see the reflection in the surface. You see only distortion, yet at the bottom all remains calm. What happens when the surface is still? Then, of course, whatever looks upon the water is reflected back like a shiny mirror, and the stillness and beauty of the entire pond is apparent. You have the power within you to still the waters of your mind. Only then, when what is at the surface matches the peace that is always at your depths, do you see the reflection of who and what you truly are.

Strive to maintain a calm surface. It is not always possible, for the wind comes and goes, whipping up the tiny wavelets. But with a deep well of peace from which to draw, you can cause an upwelling of calm from the depths and show the world your True Nature. Be a shiny reflection of peace and love, and all will come to drink at your shores.

August 12

ANSWERS AWAITING

Since time began man has questioned from whence he came. "Why am I here? Why do I exist?" Always men search outside themselves for these most basic of questions, oft leading to strife. If only those who seek would turn their focus inward, there they would find the answers awaiting.

This word "focus" is the key, for you are a focus of the one Divine Mind. And what is Mind, but consciousness … the very awareness that you exist … the Divine "I AM." As a focus—a manifestation—of the Divine Mind, you possess the same qualities. If the nature of God is goodness, kindness, and love, then these represent your true nature as well.

There is no need to look outside of yourself for these qualities in others. They are there, most certainly, but your purpose, dear ones, is to develop these qualities in yourself to the fullest … to uncover your innate divine nature. As you do so, there you will find fulfillment—in the fullness of your Self.

DREAM MAKER

Forget your dreams, for to you dreams are things which may or may not happen. You long for them to come true, but in your limited mind, you see them as an impossibility. This is a negation of your power as a spirit-being. As a focus—a manifestation—of the Creator, you are endowed with limitless creative potential. Your so-called dreams are potential not yet realized.

How do you make your dreams come true? You see them as a creation which you as a God-Being are ready to create. Having made this decision, you see your so-called dreams as reality now, and there you place your focus. You are a focus of the consciousness of the God-Force. You create your dreams—your reality—by placing your focus on that which you wish to create. And so it is.

Take away the doubt, for doubt changes the creative vibration of your thoughts and negates your efforts. Maintain the highest possible vibration. Do whatever work is necessary whilst maintaining this high vibratory focus, then watch your so-called dreams unfold. Then you will see that dreams do indeed come true, but they were never dreams. You are not a dream of the Creator, but a creation, made from love.

August 14

LIGHT AND DARKNESS

Into each life some rain must fall. This you know quite well. Your life is a series of ups and downs, highs and lows. How else would you know what light was, if not for the experience of darkness? Do not be in such a hurry to experience our world of pure light and love, for through the experience of the great polarities in your world, you grow ever so much faster in your understanding of Life.

Life is goodness. You have been given the ability to think and to create, and one of your greatest tools is choice. You can choose to see the goodness and to create more of the goodness. As a group, too many of you focus on the darkness, and thus, this is what you experience. Would you, as a mass consciousness, focus only on the light, much greater would be your experience of the light.

Each of you is like a tiny candle in the darkness. Your flame appears not to make a difference, but there you err. Imagine your flame joined with others and bringing ever more light into your world. Then, my children, the rain would cease to fall so often. You would experience the warmth of the Great Sun which always shines upon you … which waits only for you, yourself, to part the clouds.

CONSTRICTION

Headaches are a symptom ... the effect of a cause. What causes the pain, but constriction—the lack of proper flow within the brain. Fear is a constriction of the flow of Love. Love is your natural state—your very essence. When you are open and loving, your Life Force flows freely. When you perceive a threat, your thoughts do create a reaction within the physical body. Again, all is always cause and effect. If you suffer aches and pains, follow the effect back to the cause. The Great Cause is the creator of all on a macro scale. You are the creator of life on a much smaller scale, but with the same operating principles.

No one can take away the pain but yourself. No other causes you pain but yourself. You are the creator of your reality. Will you live a life of constriction, or allow the Life Force to flow freely through you? This you do control fully with your thoughts, for the Life Force is always present in abundance. Like a faucet, you control the flow. Do you restrict it to a trickle and suffer, or do you open the flood gates freely and allow it to wash through you and energize you? Call it God, call it the Life Force, or call it Love ... it is all the same Power. How much of It you experience and express is up to you.

To create harmony in your body as well as your mind, create a loving and peaceful environment within as well as without. Maintain an open flow of Love and reap the effects of what you have sown. Banish the fear and banish the pain. It is very simple ... it is the Law of Love.

August 16

SEE ONLY GOODNESS

We come to you today to speak of beauty and light. Your world carries so much darkness—a vibration which permeates your environment, passed along from generation to generation, based on cultural beliefs which have no basis in the Truth. You have wars and acts of terrorism because of a belief that these must continue. It is the collective consciousness of your body of humanity which perpetuates the killing. What would happen if suddenly all of you took on the belief that war was not a necessity … that killing is wrong … that love is all that matters?

You will not see the end of warfare or acts of killing in your lifetime, but this does not mean that you cannot make a difference. You are all cells in the body of humanity. The more cooperation amongst the cells—even if only amongst a few—little by little harmony spreads.

With an air of hopefulness … with a view for the long term—a term far longer than you will see in just this present lifetime—think and create thoughts of harmony … thoughts of love. See only goodness, and goodness will be your reality. Refuse to buy into the mass belief. Turn away from the bad news and create good news, if only on your small scale. You have no idea the beauty that can grow from one small seed.

THE ART OF ALLOWING

Disappointment … an emotion you feel when in your mind things did not go as you had planned. Yours is a world of many possibilities and limitless outcomes, yet from these outcomes you so often choose only one. Then, when it does not come to pass, you suffer. Who are you to say that the outcome you chose would have been the best? You do not see the picture from all angles. To feel disappointment is a choice. You could just as well feel nothing and be at peace. This is the art of allowing.

When you examine the circumstances, most often you will find that your disappointment arises from the actions or inactions of another. Is this not so? And how much control do you truly have over another, we ask you? Yet when another fails to act in accordance with your desires, do you not then make further attempts to manipulate them, be this by showing displeasure or by trying even harder to please? Such actions can only result in more disappointment and frustration; for once again, you cannot control another and find peace.

Peace lies only within yourself … with the realization that you are the creator of your own reality. If you wish to find that peace, allow others to walk their path in peace. The art of allowing is your path to the same destination.

August 18

TENDING THE GARDEN

The birds in the trees, the little creatures that play among the leaves on the ground, your largest mammals in the sea ... all are manifestations of Love. You and all that lives—from plants, and trees, and rocks, and all that is natural—have arisen from the Idea of God. What is God, but consciousness ... the guiding, creative, organizing Force which enlivens all that is. When you gaze upon a living thing, think to yourself, "That is God taking form." And then allow your gaze to drop to your little finger and say again, "That is God taking form." For how else would God express Itself, but through the beauty that is Life?

You, as a focus of the God Force, are endowed with the same creative ability. Your creation began with an Idea. Ideas are the seeds. Your further thoughts do cause these seeds to germinate and to grow. All that you see around you that is not a so-called natural thing, but man-made, is an example of the miracle of creation. There is not a thing that exists ... not a thing you own ... that did not begin as the seed of an idea in the mind of man, just as man began as the seed of an Idea in the Mind of God.

What will you create today? What seeds will you plant? Where will you focus your attention? Will you create tangled weeds or beautiful flowers? You are the gardener of life itself. Plant your seeds with care. Fertilize them with love and watch them grow.

YOUR GREATEST TEACHERS

When you judge another, you see not the Truth … you see only that the other is not as you are. Do you expect all others to be a mirror image of yourself? Why would God create all beings exactly alike? The Great Creator experiences life and all of its diverse aspects through Its creations. The more diverse Its creations, the more diverse and enjoyable are the experiences. Each of you brings gifts and talents and new thoughts. Each of you has your own way of experiencing creation and of creating your lives. Each of you is on your own path of experiencing Life for yourself and for your greater Self, which is that vibratory focus which you call God.

Do not judge others for their actions when they are not in accordance with your own. Send only love, for you are looking at a focus of the Divine Mind experiencing Itself. Allow each of God's creations to simply be and explore and express itself. You are not here to change another. You are here to experience your own Life. If you are unhappy with the actions or behaviors of another, then, dear ones, change yourselves.

The only thing over which you have complete dominion is your own mind. If another's actions cause you unhappiness, change your thoughts. Send only love and gratitude to those who cause you unrest, for they are your teachers. Beware of habitual reactions to your teachers, for change does not come as easily as the recognition of Who You Are. Be the model of Love, the model of allowing, and in this find the love and peace you all so badly seek.

August 20

AWAKENING

What is the awakening, but the realization that all of your life has been a lie. Do not be upset by this choice of word, for we use it only to gain your attention. There can be nothing more important in your life than awakening to the Truth that eludes some for a lifetime.

Awaken now fully to the realization that you and the Father are one. Yes, you have heard this before, yet still so many slumber. Awaken and understand that the Father is not a man in the clouds, but the Source of All That Is … the Creator. Rest assured, beloved children, that your Source is Benevolence and Love in limitless abundance. You were created from that spark of Love, to allow the Creator to enjoy Its creation. Yes, truly you were created in the Creator's image. Therefore, as you awaken to your True Nature, you discover that you need not look outside yourself for love and goodness, for you are Love and Goodness embodied … manifest in a body.

God—the Great Unlimited Force—cannot put Its arms around you, so God—your loving Father—gave you brothers and sisters with arms. Love them all and be open to their love. Feel God smile as your lips turn upward. Awake. Awake each morning and every moment with the realization that without God you would not even breathe, and that as the embodiment of God, you experience breath for God. Go forth today and love fully. Be the full expression of Spirit … fully awake and joyful in the knowledge of the Truth.

August 21

HEAL THYSELF

Healing can take place merely with thought, for thought is a power unto itself. Your thoughts have energy. If you could but see the vibrations of your thoughts, you would be quite astounded. Those thoughts of a baser level are slow and heavy, but the more loving the thought, the more fine the vibration. Have we not said many times that love is the highest vibration? Imagine, then, the effect of loving thoughts upon the body. Imagine nothing but the most refined vibrations streaming through every cell, creating one fine harmonic vibration. This is homeostasis—the perfection your body seeks.

This is the basis of your so-called spiritual healing. One who fully understands this most basic principle lays the hands upon another in which the cells are not fully in harmony. Through the hands of the healer flows the Life Force … no different than that which animates all bodies, but a strong, harmonized dose of this loving, perfect energy. All life seeks harmony, and so, when this Force is directed through a body in which there is dis-ease, the cells react with joy and rush to harmonize with this infusion of healing energy.

But hear us now: You need not seek a healer to find harmony, for all have within them the power to heal themselves. This power is your very essence. Know this and call unto you the Life Force which animates you. Call unto you a greater flow of this Force and allow it to flush out the dis-ease, bringing with it renewed health and harmony. Once infused, however, back up the healing with thoughts of self-love and love for others, for where there is nothing but love there cannot be dis-ease and pain. Heal thyself with Love … the antidote to all ills.

August 22

EXERCISE YOUR MIND

You exercise the body, but how many of you exercise the mind? Either way, it takes a discipline, and both forms of exercise result in fitness … fitness for life. Exercise of the body results in a vessel well prepared to help you fulfill your purpose in this life … to be the full expression of Spirit … to develop your divinity. Fitness of mind allows a clear and healthy expression of Spirit as well. When the mind is lazy, you fall into the trap of seeing only your material world and thinking that material things are all that matter. But matter matters little. What matters most are the things you cannot touch: kindness, compassion, understanding, and above all … love.

To think only of love and of being loving requires discipline so as to avoid the distractions of your material world. Make the decision to exercise each day … not just the body, but foremost the mind … your "exercise machine." Loving thoughts are your sit-ups. They strengthen the core. Practice them repeatedly until loving thoughts dominate all others. But just as you can never stop exercising the body or risk returning to an unfit state, you cannot grow lazy of mind, lest you be tempted to fall back into old patterns of judgment and criticism and anger, and all of the other falsehoods that keep you from being Who You Truly Are.

Exercise your mind, dear ones—not just daily, but in every moment. Strengthen your mind. Develop your spirituality with loving thoughts, and life will no longer be a contest or a competition, but a rich experience through which you sail with ease.

August 23

PIECES OF A PUZZLE

Part and parcel of the whole … that is what you are … not a separate being, but an intricate piece of the puzzle. What is a puzzle, but one great picture that is incomplete without all the pieces. Each piece by itself holds a part of the story. It brings special gifts to the picture. Each piece adds flavor and interest. You are a piece in the picture of Life … multifaceted, colorful, intriguing. You add depth and interest to the grand picture. Yet, set yourself apart from the other pieces, and what do you have? A beautiful piece, yes, but a mere fragment of the whole.

It takes all of the pieces fitting together in harmony to bring out the full beauty and the full meaning of the picture. Standing alone, you are incomplete. Find out just how you fit in the puzzle by experimenting. There is a perfect spot for you. You were created with your special facets to fit in perfectly in just the right place. It is there waiting for you, yet you need to see the big picture to understand this.

It is by serving the other pieces around you that you fit in the best. Trying to fit in without taking into consideration how you help the other pieces and the picture as a whole does lead to a bad fit. Your place awaits you. When you find it, you will know it as you click into place with precision and see the perfection. For now, recognize your innate beauty. Recognize that you are part and parcel of the whole—never forgotten … always accompanied … and always loved.

August 24

PAINT YOUR LIFE

Your world is pure energy. Everything vibrates. All of these energetic waves flow through you and around you, and all affect you in subtle (and at times not so subtle) ways. Color has its own vibration. What colors do you surround yourself with? You need not study the scientific frequency of color. You need only ask yourself, "How does this color make me feel?"

Look at the choice of color in which you clothe yourself. What does this say about you? Look at the colors of the walls in your dwelling. What do they say about you? How do these affect you? Seek always to raise your personal vibration higher and finer. You can use color to this end.

Experiment. Sense the different vibrations and how they affect your moods. You are the artist of your life, and all the world is your palette. Paint your world with colors that reflect who you truly are.

COMPASSIONATE DISPASSION

You well up with frustration when others react contrary to your liking. This is a very human response. Do not berate yourself for feeling less than loving. Simply recognize it and then shift to spirit-consciousness. From this place of love, send compassion to those who do not think as you do. What is compassion, but understanding mixed with love.

From this place of compassionate understanding you can now experience dispassion, which is not a lack of caring, but a lack of excitement. Dispassion equates with peace, and is this not the optimum place from which to face all trials?

Radiate peace-filled love, and that will be your experience.

August 26

TRUE BEAUTY

It matters not how a person looks on the outside, but how their thoughts look on the inside. True beauty lies in the thoughts. When a person houses beautiful thoughts, it matters not how the physical features are arranged or adorned, for the inner beauty gives them a radiance that cannot be denied. This radiance is like a magnet. Others are drawn to those who hold true love inside, yet often they do not even understand the attraction.

Do not place so much emphasis on outer beauty. Place your thoughts on your thoughts. This is your true make-up. Paint your thoughts with loving colors. Adorn them with the jewels of generosity and kindness. Dress them in compassion and patience, and you will be a model of such beauty that heads will turn, regardless of your exterior appearance.

The external is always changing, always subject to judgment, but that which lies inside is eternal—your spirit. The spirit is pure love and goodness at its core … always waiting for you to awaken to this Truth and let your true beauty shine. You always control the thoughts which begin within and create the external. You have no need for fancy clothes and all the things you are buying. Create beauty within and be beautiful … without even trying.

August 27

BELIEVE IN YOURSELF

How many times do you doubt yourself? You wish to do something, to accomplish some task, to achieve some goal that lies in your heart, yet your thoughts hold you back. You may blame some external cause or some physical weakness, but if you look more closely, again you will see that all that is holding you back is you. You create your reality with your consciousness. If you think you cannot achieve something, then this becomes your reality.

There is a strange phenomenon among you … you often wait to be told by others if you are capable of something—a kind of waiting to be given permission to believe in great possibilities. Once another outside of you says, "You can do it!" then, and only then, do you believe. Is this not so? Have you not witnessed this in yourself?

What if you were to become your own cheerleader? If you were not to wait for another, but to tell yourself, "You can do it! I believe in you! There is nothing you can't do!" Then, my friends, there would be nothing you could not do.

The truth is, there is nothing you can't do once you place your full belief and intention on a goal, for it is the belief and intention which hold all power. These are the tools of Consciousness … the tools of Creation. Hold yourself back no longer. Wait no longer for permission or outside encouragement. Believe in yourself. Cheer yourself on. Reclaim your Power.

August 28

LOVE WITHOUT CONDITIONS

Love unconditionally. What conditions are you placing on your loved ones? Why should you love without conditions? It is simple: because love is all you are. Call it Spirit … call it Consciousness … call it God … it is all the same energy. Love is the highest vibration of this energy. This is your Source. The higher you raise your personal vibration, the closer you become to your Source and reveal your True Nature.

When you place conditions upon the love you feel toward others, you are constricting the flow—constricting your Self. How many times a day do you look at one whom you claim to love and think, "He or she should not do this or that. He or she should not think that way, or speak that way, or act that way."? Who are you to say how another should behave or think? Each is on his own path. It is always best to concern yourself with your own soul's development.

One of the fastest ways in which you can develop your soul is by ceasing judgment of others, especially those most close to you, and sending them only love. This is loving without conditions. When you can master this key step, then you will live as The Master … a most lofty goal, but one well within your reach. Examine your thoughts. Do you truly love others, or just parts of others? True love encompasses all parts without condition.

JUST YOU WAIT

"All things come to those who wait." Another of your wise sayings, yet how many of you live by these words? Are you not always in a hurry to get somewhere where you are not? Yet when you get there, are you not already looking forward to the next goal? See again the words: "All things come to those who wait." It is in the waiting where things happen. Stop now and wait, and while you are waiting, look around you. All that you experience now while you are waiting is the result of a seed that you planted during a past moment of waiting. So do you see how very important are those moments of seed planting?

Know that all you see, and have, and experience is the result of a cause, for all is cause and effect. What you do and think in each moment—in the "now" as you say—creates your future moments without fail. It is the Law. So enjoy the "now" fully, knowing the future you are creating in the now has no choice but to materialize.

There you will find the patience to sit back and wait, knowing you have already created your envisioned future. Yes, you will need to take action to help your creations materialize, for this is how things operate in your physical realm. But take action consciously in the now, focusing on each moment, for each moment is all that matters. The future matters not. You have only and always this moment. Live it fully.

August 30

WHAT BODY?

Do not let your body stand in your way. It is a most useful tool for your purpose in life, which is to express your divinity—to express Love at all times. When you forget that that is all the body is—an instrument—then it is no longer an instrument, but an impediment.

You are not limited by the boundaries of your body. Some look upon the outer skin as the border, just like the border of a foreign nation, where you need special documents or permission to cross over. And so you remain within the boundaries of your so-called border as if trapped.

You are never trapped, except by your self-limiting thoughts. The body is not your true self. You are Pure Consciousness, created in the image of the Creator. Does the Creator have a body? Some continue to believe this myth, but it is not so. That aspect of you which is in the image of the Father cannot be seen nor touched, for it is Pure Spirit. It is your consciousness.

Consciousness has no boundaries. It has no borders, and thus no limitations. You need no special permission to travel infinite distances with your consciousness, for you are already everywhere. Once you realize this, my friends, you are truly free.

August 31

FIREFLIES

Fireflies blink on and off, and so do you. All is energy. If you could but see the continuous pulsations of all that surrounds you, to include your physical body, your entire perception of reality would change. You blink on and off with each pulsation of your electrons, but one aspect of you does not fluctuate, and that is your consciousness. This aspect of you arises from what you call "the void," but it is nothing less than the Mind of God from which all that is arises.

Where does all matter go when it blinks "off"? Back to the void, to be created a billion times yet again, until it has served its purpose. But Consciousness is eternal. Its purpose is simply to "be" and to experience. How will you use the physical matter around you to fulfill the purpose of Consciousness? Understanding that the nature of this Consciousness is goodness, you attune to your True Nature by experiencing goodness with all of your actions.

The firefly emits a light when it blinks "on." Allow the light of your spirit to shine as brightly as humanly possible whilst you blink "on" in this evanescent lifetime.

September 1

THE POWER OF FRIENDSHIP

You gather in groups for companionship. "There is safety in numbers," you say. But truly, why do you enjoy so much the company of others? It is because there you see reflected the nature of your Self. Each of you is a focus of God—a spark of the Divine. Each of you shines your light out into the world and hopefully makes your world a brighter place. Imagine each of you like a flashlight shining in different directions. And then imagine if those beams were all focused like a laser. There is the power.

That light is the love that burns inside you all. If you were to focus it together and shine it like a laser upon those who do not yet see the light, such brightness you would bring to your world.

Enjoy your friends. Friendship is a gift from God. The companionship of others allows you to enjoy God's creations just as God does. But use your companions as God does—not for pure entertainment, but to intensify God's light in the world. Go forth today, join with your friends, and shine God's light ever brightly.

September 2

BEYOND THE BODY

Never forget who you are. You are not your name. You are not the face that people recognize. You are not a butcher, a baker, or a candlestick maker. All of these titles mean nothing and actually hold you back from realizing the real you. The real you is eternal. The real you has no artificial boundaries and identities. The real you is a vibration in time and space creating a ripple that interacts with all other ripples. The only difference between you and the other ripples is not your name, not your appearance, not what you have done or labeled yourself, but the quality of your personal vibration. That vibration is what continues into eternity.

You know only a limited spectrum of vibration whilst you assume the dense body. That which is truly you vibrates so finely that you must expand beyond the physical to perceive it. This you can achieve through meditation. There you will taste the sweet nectar that requires no taste buds. There you will behold beauty beyond imagining that requires no eyes. There you will glimpse eternity. Rise above the labels and the looks. Be that which you are now, and see how your life changes.

September 3

NEW BEGINNINGS

New beginnings are always good, but they are not always welcome to you. It is all in how you see your circumstances. Do you approach change with fear and trepidation, or do you see it as the opportunity that it is to create the future of your dreams? When the life you have become accustomed to suddenly changes, you experience turmoil, for you have forgotten that nothing in your world of matter is permanent. All is in a constant state of change. Accept this fact. Allow change to be the rule rather than the exception, and there you will find peace.

Once you enter into this state of allowing, then you have created room to create excitement. And why excitement? For now you are like the artist with a blank canvas and a fresh palette. The canvas is your future. The palette is your mind with which you create your intentions and your fresh ideas. This is how you, the artist of your life, do create your ever-changing future. Your life is your masterpiece … ever changing, never the same from moment to moment, and never frightening when you control the paintbrush.

September 4

BE YOURSELF

"Be only Love" … three words which should guide every decision and every step you make. Rather than making things difficult, stop before you act. Stop before you utter a word, and think, "How would Love act?" You need not study the Masters nor read ancient texts to know the answer, for you are Love. And so, when we advise you to be only Love, we are, in truth, recommending that you be your True Self. Anything less than loving shows that you have forgotten who you are and what you are. You have bought into the false idea that you are separate from the Creator.

Be only Love. Speak only loving words. Perform only loving acts, and this shall be your experience in return. Just relax. Remember who you are. You need not put on a false front to conform. Simply be your Self and there you will find true peace.

September 5

THE ROAD AHEAD

We in the world of spirit do know what lies ahead for you in the immediate future. The longer future is less certain, for it will be affected by each tiny choice you make in each moment—by each thought which arises from your mind. (Be ever mindful that your thoughts in themselves are choices.)

As for your future, picture it as a large map spread out before you. When you chose to come to this experience in the physical realm, you chose your final destination on the map. You, as a sentient being with free will, are free to choose which route you will take.

Looking at the map of your life, there are main highways and many tiny roads. Your psychics can see the destination points and some of the main highways with their twists and turns and bumps along the way. But you in the driver's seat may suddenly choose, on a whim, to turn down one of the side roads and thus to change your experience of the journey in a way that was not foreseen. You will often know immediately when you might have chosen a better route. None of this is bad or good; it simply is. It is all part of the journey.

Know that the future is spread before you like a map, then concentrate well on your driving. Do no harm to those around you as you travel. Be courteous and kind and send them love, and your road will be all the more smooth.

September 6

JUST FIVE MINUTES

Are you dissatisfied with your life? What would you do to change it? "Anything," you say? What if we were to tell you that the change you desire would come about with the simple investment of five minutes out of each day? Would you be willing to invest five minutes to change your life? If so, then join us daily and sit quietly. Five minutes. That is all we ask. Five minutes on a regular basis of closing your eyes so as to close out the outer world and then focusing on your inner world.

Yes, of course your mind will want to chatter. Tell it you will be back in a few, but please be quiet for now. Concentrate on your slow breathing as a way of quieting your thoughts. This is the beginning. If you use these five minutes as a training ground to attune to All That Is, having the intention when you sit of getting to know yourself as the God-Force, then true change will begin. (Yes, a bold statement, we know, but how else will you transform your life?)

Are you dissatisfied with your life? Begin to change it with five minutes a day. Every day. Change will occur. It is the law of cause and effect. And if those five minutes become ten, then fifteen, then twenty, then we cannot be responsible for your transformation, for at that point you will truly begin to understand who you are, and you will finally take full responsibility for your life.

September 7

JUST ASK

You are so much greater than you have been led to believe. You are not trapped in this body. You are limitless. Once you understand this and begin to act from that place of limitlessness, then the entire universe opens up to you. Surrender. It is the ego that wishes to keep you small and limited. You are far more than this tiny thought of a person in time. You are the very God-Force at work. Harness this power and find fulfillment. Flow with it instead of against it and see how easily things fall into place.

"And how do I do that?" you ask. Just that … you ask! Make the connection in your mind with All That Is, and ask in every moment, "What's next? Guide me, please."

It is that simple.

September 8

YOUR INTERNAL COMPASS

You wander at times as if lost, wondering, "Which way should I turn?" But your life comes with no directions. You are left to interpret the map as you are. "Should I take the high road or the low? The main road or the back road? And if I do, what if I should get lost?"

Know now that inside you lies a compass. Its direction-pointing ability is unerring. Always it will lead you in the right direction. The problems begin when you look for signs outside of yourself. Beware of billboards with their glitter and bright colors. These often lead you down a dead end with their glaring temptations. Follow, instead, the ever-gentle nudging of the needle. The Compass does not speak loudly, nor poke you in the ribs. Often you will have to ask it deliberately to point the way; but because you asked, its directions are all the more clear.

Walk about today and imagine this Compass in your hand. Use it as the Divine Divining Tool that it is—leading you to water when you thirst, leading you to companionship when you are lonely, and always, my friend, pointing the way Home when you are lost.

September 9

YOUR MINISTRY

Each of you has a ministry. You minister unto others when you take the time to care for them more than yourself. The self is so very self-absorbed. This you call the ego. Do not denigrate the ego, for it plays a very important role. It allows you to fulfill your purpose in life by exposing the ego for what it is—a disguise you wear temporarily over your True Self. It is your task first to recognize this disguise and then to remove it piece by piece until your True Self is fully revealed—that part of you which is all goodness, all kindness, all compassion … all Love.

When you minister unto another, you are allowing your True Self to shine through your ego. That part of the other person that may or may not yet be awakened cannot help but sense this light in you and stir. Today, may you be a minister. May you give the ego a rest and help others to see their Light.

September 10

THIS EVER-PRESENT MOMENT

As you travel down the road, you see yourself passing by all of the things around you. Is this illusion, or is it real? Change your perspective as you gaze at the road. Imagine, instead, that you are perfectly still and the road is passing under your feet. The scenery is flying by you. In actuality, this is much closer to how your life operates than you know. Your sense of time, with your past, present, and future, is much like this analogy. You did not live in the past. You will not live in the future. You live only now—in this moment. The past is what has flown past you. The future will be passing by. But you do not move.

You stand here in this moment, free to create whatever you want from this moment. You have allowed the past to shape your beliefs. You cling to your memories as if they are real things. The past is gone. It has flown by you. It holds no more meaning, nor does the future. All meaning lies in this moment alone. You are not a victim of your past, nor paralyzed by what lies ahead. You are all powerful in this moment.

Seize this moment and enjoy it fully, unaffected by moments long flown by. Who you are now is who you will always be—an expression of all goodness. Use that goodness to create more goodness. Be the presence of love here, now, in the present, which is all you ever have.

September 11

GOOD FOR THE SOUL

You wish to laugh? You wish for words of wit? Why do you think this is? Why does laughter feel so good to you? It is because it is all part of that Power which flows through you, which is all goodness.

Do you not see that you are here to be an expression of that which you call God? And do you not think that this Power enjoys your joy? While God is neither a man nor a woman, God shares the same mind as man and woman, for there is, in reality, only One Mind. From where comes humor, then, do you think? Is it purely a human trait? From where comes the human, then, we ask you? All things arise from the Mind of God. Do you not think, then, that God has a sense of humor?

God takes great pleasure in seeing you laugh, for God cannot laugh. You are the expression of God. Humor, when used to bring joy, can be as a balm to the soul. Jokes used to bring a bit of light to another's life are yet one more of the tools God has given you to bring more light into your world. Humor is yet another way to reveal the light in a world with far too much darkness. You are here to reveal your own light. Look for ways to laugh, and there you will find another avenue into your soul.

September 12

LIKE A BOOMERANG

When others do not think as you do, when others complain or make a fuss where you would not have, this does tend to ruffle your feathers. This kind of reaction in yourself is habitual. Habits can be broken. If you find that you habitually react to others who differ from you with disdain or scorn, the first step is to recognize this. The second is to thank them for the lesson. The third is to release the judgment. Once you release these negative thoughts which keep you feeling as separate entities, you can begin to view the other as no different than yourself.

Do you not think that you have habits that irk others? None of you is perfect. Would you not appreciate it if others looked upon you without judgment and simply sent you love and acceptance? Of course this is not your current reality, but it is a laudable goal. In the meantime, you can practice this for yourself, for what you display in your thoughts and actions is what comes back to you more and more.

If you have a neighbor or an acquaintance whom you find troublesome—whom you turn away from every time you see them in the distance out of a desire to avoid interaction, stop yourself and approach them on purpose. Change your habitual reaction to this person. Send them love and understanding, then let it go. Do not expect to perceive a change in behavior from this other, but you can expect to be treated in the same manner by someone else, now that you have sent this energy outward. It is the law. You say, "What goes around comes around," and there is much truth in this. So go around without judgment, sending only love, and allowing others to be as they are. Like a boomerang, your love will come back to you, so let the boomerang fly.

September 13

REACTIONS

"Did you meet the situation with love?" That is the great test of your lifetime. This is a test you can apply after any event, any experience. And apply it you should, for it will be the question you are asked by your higher self and by those who gently guide you when you pass through heaven's gate.

Yes, your life is filled with challenges, and always you do have a choice of how to respond. So many ways do you have from which to choose. You can respond with fear, with anger, with defensiveness ... by running away, by taking a stand, or by doing nothing. All is a spectrum from low vibration to high. Understanding this, you can see that the optimum choice is always love. We challenge you to find any circumstance when love is not the optimum choice.

When faced with a choice, step into the future and look back upon the moment. Did you meet the moment with love? Constant vigilance, my friend. Constant vigilance.

September 14

THE SIGN AROUND YOUR NECK

All of your needs are provided. This you have heard over the years, and yet you see the beggar on the corner with his sign. And where is his provision? Why do some go homeless and without food? It is because they are living in darkness. Call it ignorance, if you will. It is all the same … a lack of understanding of the true power of the human being. The human being is not the limited creature those in darkness see it to be, but Spirit through and through. Once you understand this, then all abundance is yours.

True abundance is Love. You are given a limitless supply of this creative power. "Love cannot create money," you say, but this is not true. When there is famine or natural catastrophe, does not the money flow? And where does this flow originate? From love.

You, as a manifestation of the Great Creative Force can create the life you wish. Read the beggar's sign. His words there define the limited life he has created. Were he to change his thoughts and his view of his creative power, he could never hold such a self-limiting sign. Emboldened with new thoughts derived from his Power, oh, how his life would change. It is the same for you. What sign do you hang around your neck? By your actions and your circumstances, are you telling the world you are a limited being, or the limitless expression of God's love?

September 15

IT'S ALL IN THE ASKING

Ask and you shall receive. This is the way your world works. "But I have asked quite often and see no results," you say. Let us explain. First, please understand that you must pay attention to how you ask. Be most deliberate in your wording. Quite often you will receive exactly what you ask for.

Second, have patience. There may be quite a delay between the asking and the receiving. You may have lessons to learn first—bricks to put in the wall of your life that you are building. You cannot lay the top row before the others have been laid. When finally you do receive, you will look back and see the perfection.

And lastly, always what you receive will serve the greater good, for all is One. So when we say, "Ask and you shall receive," we are not talking about a new car, or house, or other ephemeral material possession. Ask for those things which will awaken your soul and help your Light and the Light of those around you to shine ever brighter. These prayers are always answered in time. It is the Law, and God's laws cannot be broken. So, ask away.

September 16

TRUE POWER

Why does it matter who or what you are? Are titles and labels so important? Look at those who cease to work and suffer great depression at the perceived loss of their identity. This is ignorance—ignorance of your greatest Truth.

You need no labels or titles to be the most powerful person on your earth. But understand us well—our definition of power may differ from yours. If to you power means money, recognition, and adulation, then you, too, will suffer from this depression when the false idols disappear. But when to you power comes to mean love and the ability to connect with others through the heart—at a soul level—then you will see that at this very moment you are all-powerful.

Set aside all labels and titles you use to identify yourself and to differentiate yourself from all others. Focus instead on your true and everlasting Power, and there find the peace that all men seek.

September 17

PUPPY LOVE

Have you ever had a puppy lick your face? Then you have experienced pure love … love without conditions. In that simple gesture you felt the flow of goodness and acceptance of who you are, with no concern for what you may have done in the past or what you had to give. Puppies wish only to show you how very special you are to them.

This kind of love is yours to give as well. It is far from the human kind of puppy love, which is all chemicals and selfish needs. Be as the puppy. See in others only loveable beings who need your love, and give it to them as a smile, as a hug, as a loving phrase, or as a beam of radiant love-energy, expecting nothing in return.

You can teach an old dog new tricks. It matters not how old you are. Be as the puppy and bring a smile to all you meet today.

September 18

ALONE VS. LONELY

Cherish the moments you spend by yourself. So often you try to fill the time with noise. The television or radio plays in the background as if to blot out the silence. Of what are you afraid? Of hearing your own thoughts? Of getting to know yourself? What is so bad about this word "alone"? Do you see the basis of this word when you separate the syllables? "Alone" becomes "all one." You are never truly alone, for all are interconnected. There is only one Mind… one Spirit … and you are It.

Why do you run from loneliness? It is because, beloved one, you are living with a false sense of separation. Something in your past to which you cling continues to hold you prisoner as if in a lonely cell. The bars are imaginary. Know this well. You can bend the bars as if butter and free yourself in an instant. See that the world is full of souls who all enjoy thc same emotions as you.

You wish to be like those who are completely at peace while seemingly alone? Call forth within you that part of All One that is pure Love, for this is the essence of Oneness. Do this, and you will find yourself actively seeking to be al-one.

September 19

PENNIES FROM HEAVEN

Pick a penny from the ground
Then rejoice in what you found.
To you this little treasure
Holds worth beyond its measure.

To most its value is one cent.
It buys not much when it is spent.
But the fun is in the finding,
For this treasure is reminding

That always there does lie a gift
Ready for your mind to lift.
Scattered there like copper leaves—
A sign from God, for he who believes.

"In God We Trust" is written there,
A clear reminder for those who care
To read these words and thus to know
That God is there where 'ere you go.

So when next you find a penny lost
That perhaps for luck was tossed,
To you the luck does come in turn
When the penny's simple lesson you do learn.

FREE FLOWING

Blockages. We speak of them often. And you do ask, "Blockages of what?" Blockages of that which animates you—of the Life Force. This Life Force flows through you at all times, for if not, you would not survive in this world. You would pass to our world of pure spirit.

So how do you block this flow? Quite simple—with your thoughts. Your thoughts and your imagination are the prime movers of God-energy. When thoughts are limited, such as those which are unkind or unloving to yourself or others, the Life Force is limited.

To truly feel alive and vibrant, search for the ways in which your thoughts limit the flow. Blame no others. Look inside. You create the dams and you can knock them down. Expand your thoughts with love for yourself and others. Feel the vitality, energy, and yes—Life—return to your veins as this vitalizing Force is given free rein by your mind to flow.

September 21

WHERE TRUE POWER LIES

Competition and cooperation—two words which begin with similar letters, but on a spectrum are as far apart as they can be. What is competition, but the purest evidence that there exists a sense of separation. And why do two people compete? For the ego's need to prove just how separate it is. The ego needs to feel powerful, and what better way to do so, than to beat the chest and say, "Watch me try to be better than you."

But is one being truly better than another? "Never," is the answer. All are unique—yes, endowed with certain gifts and abilities, but never better in the eyes of God. Turn competition into cooperation, and all of the abilities can be combined to produce far greater results than when kept separate through illusion. Set aside the ego. See the oneness, and cooperate. In this there is no end to the goodness you can create.

September 22

YOUR LIFE RAFT

Further effort is not always necessary when you begin to achieve success on a project. Know that evidence of success is a sign that you are in the flow. That is to say, that your mind and thoughts are working in harmony with the higher good and that all is in order. Once you recognize this state of positive flow, relax and trust. Flow has momentum. As long as your thoughts continue in the same vein, then all that is necessary is simply to trust in the nature of Life.

When there are positive thoughts and intentions, goodness and order follow. Struggle and exertion are not necessary. Relax, trust, and float in the direction of the flow, as if on a raft. This is the Life raft, and always it will keep you afloat and drifting with unerring accuracy in the direction of your destiny.

September 23

HERE AND NOW

There are those who are always waiting … waiting for something better to come along. They are never satisfied with their current circumstances. Can you not see from your vantage point that they will never be satisfied? For them, satisfaction lies in something that has not yet happened.

Are you sometimes guilty of the same thing? Step outside of yourself and have a look. What do you see? One who is always striving, hoping, and looking forward or one who is perfectly content with their life now? If not the latter, then slow down a moment. Put on the brakes and stop time, for time is only an illusion. This "someday" that you long for will never get here. It will always remain "someday." Yes, the things you long for may arrive in the present moment, but "someday" will remain ever illusive.

Sit back in your stopped state and take stock of this moment. Can you be satisfied with what you have here and now? If not, then change your "here and now" here and now. "Here" is where change happens. "Now" is all you ever have. Live it fully, my friend. Immerse yourself in the joy of simply "being," being ever grateful for the never-ending moments of now.

September 24

THE NEVER-ENDING CYCLE

Growing old is never easy, as you watch your loved ones depart from this world … as you watch the changes in your body and theirs … but is not all of life about change? You have seen the changes in the seasons your whole life. All of life expresses itself in cycles—cycles of nature: birth, growth, aging, death … a never-ending cycle.

You watch the leaves appear, grow, turn green, then brown, then flutter to the ground to return to the earth from which they came, only to return again with the next season. Your life is but a mirror of this process. You fear aging and death. These are inevitable. This you know. But have no fear. Your spirit participates in the same cycle as the leaf and of all things.

You will die to this current experience, but many experiences lie ahead of you and those you love. Always remember, where two are linked by the bonds of love, always will they be joined—here and hereafter. Say goodbye for now, but in the great cycle of life, there is always another reunion.

September 25

ANOTHER WORLD

You look with dread upon the dead,
Thinking it's the end.
But there is far more to this life.
This message we do send:

Do not think that what you see
Is truly what is real.
Nor are the things you hear and taste,
Nor are all things you feel.

The physical it does not last.
Its permanence is fleeting.
This truth you'll learn quite clearly
When passed loved ones you are greeting.

Another world exists beyond
The one in which you live.
But you can feel its presence now
If your attention you do give.

Sit quietly and ask to know
The world beyond yourself.
And then to you will come a sense
Of treasure beyond wealth.

A greater sense of knowingness
Will be your great reward.
For stepping out and trusting,
God's bright light you're drawn toward.

For now relax and trust our words
As your reality expands.
For trust is what this path you're on
So frequently demands.

We praise you for your efforts.
They never are in vain.
So sit with us and worship
And much greatness you will gain.

September 26

FLIP THE SWITCH

Forgiveness … a topic which arises quite often in our lessons, for yes, it is one of the lessons so many of you struggle with the most. Forgiveness is a gift. It is a form of surrender, but not a form of weakness. When you can sit back and release all blame, holding nothing but love for another, then you have given the greatest gift possible to yourself. You harm not the other when you withhold your love, for they are already the expression of God-as-Love. But you most certainly harm yourself by blocking the full expression of your Self.

Forgive yourself first and foremost when you hold resentment toward another. Bring in your light to shine upon the darkness of your ignorance. In the fullness of your new understanding, forgive yourself, for no other truly does you wrong—you merely perceive it as such. All is interpretation.

When you can forgive another, you make room for light to enter your own soul. It takes but an instant. You struggle so long, but all you need do is flip the switch and turn on the light.

September 27

FOCUS

Where you place your focus is what you bring to yourself. It is the Law. So sit and ask yourself, "What do I wish to manifest in this life?" By the same token, take notice when things you do not desire in your life continue to manifest. What is it in your thoughts that are bringing these people and situations to you? What is it in your focus that is maintaining the presence of that which you no longer want or need?

Do not blame forces outside yourself for that in your life which brings you displeasure. All that you have and are is the result of your focus. Thoughts are so very important, and you control them all. Bring your thoughts into focus and take control of your life.

September 28

YOUR GREATEST ROLE

All of life is the play of Light—God's Light. You are an actor in this play—not a puppet on strings, but one chosen for a most important role: to express the grand ideas of the play's Producer. At times you distance yourself from the Producer and play your part as you see fit. When not in accordance with the grand design of the production, chaos erupts on the stage. This affects not just you, but other actors and the props as well. When you play your part as the Producer intended, awards lie in store.

So how do you win the grand prize? Ask the Producer to define your role. Have you had a one-on-one talk with Him lately? He is not a hands-off Director. Invite him to guide you as you act out your role in this grand play of life, and the stage will be well set.

FOR ONE WHO IS SUFFERING

A fellow human being
Who walks upon the earth
Feels the same emotions
Which you have felt from birth.

You think that you're alone
As you struggle and you toil,
But all do face the same great tests
As they walk upon the soil.

No human is exempt from pain.
No one does go without
The sorrows and the loss you feel.
Of this there is no doubt.

So when you face a challenge great,
Just know you're not alone.
Help is there awaiting you
By those who also pain have known.

Pull not inside and hide your fears
When worries come apace.
Turn instead to others,
Then your troubles you can face.

Your world is filled with loving souls
Who walk the self-same path as you.
God's gift to man in human form—
Love that comes to see you through.

September 30

PERFECT ALREADY

Perfection is not so easily attained, yet you strive for this. The goal is not a bad one, but the trouble comes when you fail to achieve this ever-elusive state and feel somehow less than you are.

At your essence, you are perfect already. You are perfect love, for your Source is pure love. You have accepted this lifetime experience in order to express this divine nature. If, in striving to be perfect, you strive to be the perfect expression of love, all else will fall into place. Your life will flow divinely. Miracles will be the norm. However, if you strive to have the perfect house, the perfect car, the perfect clothes, the perfect yard, and your life is not flowing as you think it should, then retreat to the basics.

These external elements (the house, the car, the yard …) can be yours and oft-times land in the lap even when priorities have been skipped over. But all of these physical trappings lose their luster when you discover the part of yourself that can shine brighter than any fine stone or new car. If you must be a perfectionist, then perfect your loving thoughts and actions. All else will follow.

October 1

NO LIMITS

Step outside of yourself. This we have told you before. But what do we mean? You allow your body to define your boundaries. To so many, the world of awareness ends at the skin, but this is an illusion. The body is a vessel—true—but you exist far more around and beyond the body than within it. The body allows you to experience the physical world and to interact with this world, but do not allow the body—as so many do—to cut off your experience of your eternal existence as a spirit-being. You are that ethereal energy being now. Expand your consciousness and you expand your self-imposed limits.

Your consciousness … your mind … your spirit is pure energy. As such, it has no boundaries. Visualize yourself without limits, and the spectrum of new experiences and knowledge to which you will be exposed will amaze you. "What was I waiting for? Why did I not do this and know this earlier?" You may find yourself asking these questions when you discover that this part of yourself has been there all along. You were waiting for just the right moment, and the moment is now.

Welcome home.

October 2

LIFT-OFF

Birds do fly and soar, enjoying what appears to be far greater freedom than you with the heavy physical body which keeps you so firmly rooted to the ground. But make no mistake ... You can soar like a bird as well. To gain your wings and fly, first realize what you are: a spirit-being, a child of the Great Spirit, which has decided to walk as man or woman for a short while and experience legs and feet. Inside that man or woman lies a pulsing, vibrant spirit.

Can you not feel it? Can you not hear it whispering to you in those times when you pull your concentrated focus back from the body and all that the body senses? It is then you find your wings. It is then, in the realization that you are only temporarily using this body to experience an aspect of reality, that you experience lift-off.

Detach from your great attachment to all things physical, and fly, my friends. Soar as the spirit-being you are, and find the freedom to be your true Self—an expression of Love ... a spark of the Divine. Express that part of you which is divine. Express your loving nature at all times, and see just how free you truly are.

SEEKERS

Fortune seekers … those who take great risks in hopes of gaining great treasure. Always there is the excitement of anticipation that they will finally "hit it rich" and never again have to worry. But even for those who do find gold, although they may have much physical comfort and beautiful surroundings, does their worry ever cease?

Are you a seeker? If so, you already have an inkling, or perhaps even the certainty, that the Treasure lies within. So we ask you to ask yourself, do you still worry? If the answer is yes, then we ask you now to ask why you are still seeking.

Rather than always searching for more and more answers … rather than always seeking gold when Gold is what you are, be not the seeker, but be that which you seek. Be the Love you look for in others and you shall have it. Instead of always seeking, see now the Truth that has always been and will always be.

October 4

FAITH

The lesson for today is faith. There is a world of difference between the physical world in which you now walk and the world of pure spirit. Your scientists may try as they might to prove the existence of a spirit world, but always they will meet with failure, for there exist no instruments in your world, nor yet the technology to measure our frequency.

There are many among you who communicate with our world quite regularly, yet your scientists scoff at this. They cannot replicate repeatedly the results of these communications. For them, this is the only test of truth.

Your scientists may tell you that the universe was created without a God, and to this we advise you to ask yourself, "Who created you?" Yes, your parents, through a biological act did create the body which you use to express your Self, but who created that Self? When did it begin and when will it end? We can give you all the answers your scientists deny. That "Who" is the Force inside the body who knows the Truth.

Keep the faith.

October 5

SHIFTING REALITIES

Your loved ones on the other side watch over you. This, many of you suspect, but you look for proof. "How can you prove that which you cannot touch?" This, the skeptics ask. But those of you more prone to sensing, those of you who understand the meaning of faith and the joy that comes with trusting your inner guidance, do know the truth—that this is but one reality among many.

When you pass from this lifetime and leave the physical body behind, as some of your dear loved ones have done, you will experience another aspect of reality. You can touch this world now in your mind, for consciousness is the common link between all realities.

How can you prove a dream? You cannot. You can only say to others, "But it seemed so real!" This physical world seems so real to you now that here you place all faith and trust. Trust us in this: When you pass to the other side and enjoy a most loving reunion with those you so long to see again, then you will look back upon this life to which you gave so much importance and say, "But it seemed so real!"

It is real to you now, so live this life to its fullest, being the presence of Love which you are in every moment. But know that your loved ones watch over you now and await the moment when reality shifts yet again.

October 6

ON CRITICISM

Criticism ... a deeper, more harmful form of judgment. When you judge, you are looking at another and saying, "You and I are separate." When you judge, you see the differences instead of that which binds you—the Spirit, which is pure love at its essence.

Criticism is far more insidious than mere judgment. In addition to maintaining the illusion of separation, criticism says, "My way is the only way, and I disallow you to experience and act out Life in your way." In this way, you cut off your own flow of Love. You do no harm to the other, save from disallowing them the experience of your love. But trust us in this: every time you restrict your own flow, you fail to grow.

Do not miss an opportunity to be the Loving Presence that you are. Do not miss an opportunity to fulfill your presence in life, which is to be that loving presence. Suspend judgment, eschew criticism, and simply allow all of Life to unfold.

October 7

CREATING CASTLES

You see castles in the sky
Yet know not why.
They are there for the taking
For it is you who are making
These images appear
From far and near ...

You are a creator. Never underestimate your ability to create your dreams. So many sit back and wish for things they lack, thinking falsely that these things lie beyond their reach. Yet others seem to always be surrounded by success. Why is this, you ask? If you could examine the thoughts of the two people—see into their minds—you would find two very different experiences.

What you feed your mind comes out as physical reality. Feed your mind thoughts of lack and worry, and lack and worry are what you experience. What is it you wish to experience? Wait for no other to bring it to you, for they cannot. You hold the recipe for what concoctions you create. Your thoughts are the individual ingredients. The great meal upon which you feast is yours and only yours for the making.

October 8

WELCOME THE SUNRISE

We wish to congratulate you on another day of living. Your very presence here—the fact that you opened your eyes this morning—reveals the desire of your soul to grow. If you had no more lessons to learn here on earth, you would have no reason to repeat yet another day.

Rejoice in the sunrise, for the light reveals all of the beauty which is there for you to appreciate. Do not waste a moment of this day. See and appreciate the beauty around you. Count your many blessings. Be a light unto others, and further your own growth by doing so. It is that simple.

What do we mean by growth? The constant raising of your consciousness, bringing it ever more in alignment with the Divine Mind—that pure, loving, creative Consciousness from which springs your soul. When in alignment, your life flows beautifully. May you welcome the sunrise each morning, then go forth and create the most beautiful expression possible of your Self.

October 9

UNDER PRESSURE

Take a cap off of a bottle and hear the hiss of escaping air. What causes this eruption, but a build-up of pressure under the lid. And do you not do the same thing? Do you not at times open your mouth and emit a loud hiss? The hiss at times comes out as venomous words aimed to strike at another. This outburst is but a release of pressure which has built up inside of you.

Do you not immediately feel remorse? This is because the hissing and striking out goes against your true nature as a loving expression of the Divine Mind. The pressure is the build-up of thoughts which are not in alignment with your true Self.

You can avoid the outbursts altogether by a constant monitoring of your inner state, which is always caused by your thoughts. Are you beginning to boil inside? Let off the steam through healthy outlets before you burst. Say your prayers. Go for a walk. Visualize a peaceful scene. Ask for help. All of these are ways to return to a state of peaceful equilibrium. Self-monitor the pressure, and the outbursts will decrease until peace is your constant companion.

October 10

REST AND WORSHIP

The day you call Sunday … the name is merely a convenience to mark the passage of moments. One day is no different than another. One moment is no different than the next. But this "Sunday" is special to many, for they have chosen this day to rest and to honor that Power which created the world. It is a good thing to rest, and it is a good thing to worship, but do not fail to do these things every day of your life—not just when a day on a calendar reads "Sunday."

Why is rest important? It helps you to stop and "be," rather than always "doing." And why is worship important? The Great Spirit does not need your adoration. The Great Spirit has no needs at all. But if in worshipping you stop and recognize the Infinite Power that brings order to chaos and brings love where there is fear, then worship is a worthy effort. Worship not that part of you that is divine, but recognize it and give thanks for the Self-recognition.

From Sunday to Sunday go forth with gratitude and be that loving Power. Express your true nature … the only activity from which you need never take rest.

October 11

KNOWING RIGHT FROM WRONG

You can kill the body, but you cannot kill the soul. The spirit is eternal. When one takes the life of another deliberately, there is always payment at a soul level. Judgment comes not from a vengeful deity, but from within the self-same soul. Judge not another, for others will judge themselves when shown the full effect of their actions.

Much that you consider wrong is the result of ignorance—ignorance of the very nature of Life and of the Great Spirit. All of life is the expression of the God Force. Killing and mayhem are the willful uses of this force gone awry. Why is there such disharmony when these acts occur? For the soul knows wrong from right.

Those who do not see the difference between right and wrong while here in physical form will most certainly see it when they pass over and review their life. When understanding comes, so also comes the great urge to do better and to express in a far greater way the True Spirit. Souls may become temporarily lost, but all eventually find their way home. Meanwhile, maintain hope for mankind and be a model of loving kindness.

October 12

FOOD FOR THE SOUL

"There is nothing new under the sun" – yet another of your expressions. Nothing that we say to you here may strike you as new or novel. In fact, much may seem quite repetitious. There is a method in our madness. Through the repetition, the ideas are cemented in your consciousness. For most of your lives you have been feeding your subconscious with beliefs that did not bolster the soul, but the ego, instead. It is time now to feed the soul.

Nothing new here may be said, yet does the soul not hunger for these tidbits, doled out with love, just when you need them most? The words feed the hunger, for the soul knows exactly the nourishment it needs. Just as your body is made of proteins and fats, it needs more of the same to grow. And just as your soul is love and goodness at its essence, it grows through feeding it thoughts of goodness and love—by feeding it the very vibration of love which grows simply by reading these words.

It matters not if the words are new or if they have been heard a thousand times … the vibrations they set in motion within the soul are like chocolate to the taste buds. Feed well on these vibrations. No need for a diet here, beloved. Feast away on the love … the only ingredient of which the soul can never get or give enough.

October 13

COME OUT OF YOUR SHELL

"Homebound" … a word you use for those who must remain within the boundaries of a physical dwelling. Some feel trapped in this state, for they cannot exercise their freedom to get out and about and interact with the world. Many are homebound in a different sense and do not realize it. The physical body is your temporary home whilst enjoying this physical existence. Those who see it as the border of their existence often hide inside it like a turtle in a shell. They withdraw into the perceived safety of the body, averting the eyes, clamping shut the mouth, and thus closing the doors to the outside world.

The body is a communication tool. Could you but see that you as a spirit-being are not trapped at all, but are in fact constantly interacting with all that is, you would not be so quick to retreat inside. Your True Self is a loving being, as is that of every other soul on earth. When you use the physical body to separate yourself and close off the conscious interaction, you cheat yourself of the conscious experience of love. At a soul level, one soul greets another and says, "Hail, Brother! I love you. I will see you later, when this deluded being sheds its shell. Until then, be well."

Allow your spirit to be free now. Do not make it wait to fully express its loving nature. Come out of your shell. Look another in the eye and say aloud, "Hello, my friend. I love you. Thank you for being in my life. How may I help you today?" Be not homebound, but set yourself free with love.

October 14

FULLY SECURE

"Insecurity" … a word with which most humans are familiar. We speak not of physical safety, but of emotional neediness. You do experience a state of fear quite often with a basic question at the heart of it: "Do others love me?" You can break this down into a variety of lesser vibrations: "Do others like me, appreciate me, approve of me, find me attractive, interesting, and worthy?" All of these speak loudly of fear, and do lead to this non-secure feeling.

Do you not realize that others' approval of you is unnecessary? Do you not realize that you are always worthy of love and admiration? Why? Because you are a child of God—a perfect and perfectly loveable spirit-being first and foremost. Others could throw rocks and stones or verbal epithets at you repeatedly and do no harm to the spirit.

Erect the armor of love. Let this armor be not a barrier, but a shining suit you wear that reflects the light inside. Let others say what they want … think what they want. Wearing the shield of love, be perfectly secure in the knowledge that you are fully worthy. How could you be anything else?

October 15

BEYOND THE BRAIN

Whether near or far, your loved ones are never any farther than your thoughts. Do you hear the chime of a bell when someone comes to your door? This is like unto what we experience when you think of us in our world of pure energy. You—as a spirit-being in your physical world—have the benefit of a spirit-body and a physical body. Those who have crossed to our realm have only the spirit-body, but less is far more in this case. Without the impediment of the dense vibrations of physical matter interfering with thought vibrations of the spirit-body, we are free to manifest our thoughts far faster.

If you can train the brain to be quiet now and then, you can access our world with the mind—keeping in mind that the brain and the mind are quite separate. It is in these moments when you step beyond the boundaries of the brain that you experience a bit of what awaits you. For now, rest assured that in the eternal minds of those you love who have made the transition, you remain ever on their minds. They are not near and not far, but wherever you are. Send them loving thoughts and you are speaking their language. Your loving words become an embrace. Your walk down Memory Lane in your mind is a tangible visit from our point of view. You cannot waste a thought, for it is there that your loved ones reside.

October 16

WHEN IT ITCHES

What is an itch, but an irritation—a knocking at the door of your consciousness that something needs attention. "Scratch me," it says. "Take care of me now." It is a physical attention-grabber, but are you not given mental itches throughout your day?

Pay attention to the subtle itches in your mind. What are they saying to you? You will find these gentle nudges are reminders to express your loving nature. "Excuse me," the itch will say, "but perhaps you could be a bit more understanding of that other's circumstances …" And when you scratch this gentle itch, do you not see relief for both you and the other?

This inner itch is the voice of your soul, reminding you of what is truly important in life. In what you call the "real world," you apply creams and ointments to squelch the itch—balms which only treat the effect and not the cause. In your spiritual awareness, remain ever vigilant for that inner itching and respond—not by covering up the itch—but by expressing the source of that itch, which is always love.

NO NEED TO CRY

Babies cry when they need attention. Some things do not change as you grow older. Do you not cry out for attention, only not necessarily always with tears? So many acts which are contrary to your true nature as the expression of Spirit are merely cries for attention. Substitute the word "love" for "attention." Is this not what all who act angrily, fearfully, or rudely are crying out for?

If you at times are guilty of such transgressions, you need merely look inside and there you will find the source of all you are crying for. The fear, anger, and rudeness mask the love and constrict its flow. Remove these blockages, and you will find that you have no further need to cry. You are now free to dry the tears of others and free them of their constriction.

What goes around does truly come around again and again. Ensure that what goes around is love, and watch it come around to you.

October 18

THE UPS AND DOWNS OF LIFE

Behold the ever-changing landscape of your life. What you first traversed as mountains, over time and distance flattened into smaller hills with fewer valleys. Some day, as you continue along your path, you will walk quietly through fields of fragrant flowers, traveling with ease. This is the path of life, and rarely is it easy going. Quite often you do stumble, but always do you pick yourself up and continue on. The bruises and the aches do fortify you, for you learn in this way just how strong you really are.

If your path were straight and easy going from the start, you would not grow nearly as strong nor be able to recognize your growth as you have from the more challenging road you have chosen. While you may not enjoy your steps as you climb the mountains, rejoice when you reach the summit. Enjoy the glorious view, but while you are there, lean down and give your hand to another who is still climbing.

Do not fear that yet another valley lies ahead. There will always be peaks and valleys whilst you traverse this ever-changing landscape. This is the very nature of your journey. With this awareness, journey on and revel in the change, for what does it mean, but that you are alive!

October 19

ETERNAL PATIENCE

Those who are impatient do not truly understand the truths of the spirit. Impatience is an attribute of your world only—for only in your world do you experience time and the false illusion that there is not enough time. In our world, time is of no consequence. If you could step outside the bonds of the body and see the perfection—how each piece of the puzzle fits with precision into the next—you would have no need for this word "patience." You would know that all is in perfect order, and that what you need is coming to you perfectly.

When you find yourself acting impatiently, be grateful for this recognition. It is a reminder that you have forgotten who you are—an eternal spirit-being—and you have forgotten to trust. Remind yourself, "There is always enough time," and surrender your angst. There, in the absence of rushing and demands which you have placed upon outcomes, you will find the doorway to peace … the doorway to your soul, which is infinite and infinitely patient with you.

October 20

ORDER AMIDST THE CHAOS

Watch the weather patterns. See how they change and how unpredictable they are when you look any farther forward than a few days of your time. Yet, even in the unpredictability, do you not also see patterns? Your weather repeats itself in predictable cycles … reliable patterns which allow you to plan and give you a bit of a sense of security. You are frightened by howling winds, black skies, and raging waters, but are these not always followed by a gentle calm and the emergence of the sun?

All of Life exhibits order such as you see in your weather. All of Life is a series of predictable cycles. There is a Divine Intelligence bringing order to all Life. You are part of that Intelligence.

When your life seems chaotic and out of control … when storms rage inside you … know that amidst the chaos there is order. Were this not so, all would disintegrate completely. When darkness befalls you, know that you are an integral part of Life and that the sun will truly rise again.

October 21

THAT WHICH HAPPINESS BRINGS

Two cars, a house, and a cat—
Can you imagine a life like that?
It seems to be the American dream,
But are those inside as content as they seem?

Be wary of placing great value on things.
Know, instead, that which happiness brings.
It's the spirit inside that is with you right now—
Waiting to take a theatrical bow.

"It is I who your attention does seek.
Here all along, if you only would peek.
I require no money, no lavish attention.
Just your desire to know me, may it be your intention."

Knowing this, you can find what you seek in your heart—
That feeling that money will never impart.
It's the secret of life, yet just waiting for all.
The gifts of the spirit await those who do call.

Set aside all your treasures and then you will see
That even with nothing, quite rich can you be.
For love is the thing that lies at your core.
It is there for you, waiting, when you knock at its door.

October 22

MONEY FLOWS

Money flows as does your breath—ever in and out. When you hold your breath, soon you gasp and need to take in more. When you hold onto your money, afraid to spend it, you are expressing fear. Money is energy, as is all else in your world. Allow it to flow in and out of your life freely—without constriction—and you will never be without.

Abundance is the natural state of life. There is enough of all that you need. It is only your false beliefs which you have accepted as truths concerning the availability of money which cause fear to arise. Release the fear and see the money flowing in and out freely. Spend it with happiness, knowing that all you need is always provided, and so it shall be. Examine your thoughts and fears. At the same time, bring to the surface the truths you have learned about spirit and energy, and about your ability to create your desires with your thoughts.

You are an expression of the Creator. If you wish to have abundance, banish all thought of lack and create the positive flow of abundance. What you see around you is what you have created with your thoughts. Create anew in every moment. You are far richer than you ever imagined.

October 23

BE THE SPARK

Repetition is a necessary element of learning. Do not your beliefs become cemented in the subconscious mind through repeated exposure? For many years you have told yourself the same falsehoods—that you are a separate individual with no connection to those around you. And so it is that we now repeat to you the truths of the Spirit.

You are naught but energy—a vibrating wave of consciousness. If you could see this energy, you would not need the repetitious message. You would realize immediately how very intertwined is your energy with all others. It is impossible to separate that which you call "you" from "them." What you do and think affects all others. Your thoughts, beliefs, and subsequent actions become part of the Whole.

You complain about the state of the world. You think you cannot make a difference. Hear us as we repeat and repeat this truth: All is One. There is only one Mind and you are a focus of that one Divine Consciousness. To raise the vibration of the whole, begin with yourself. You can and do make a difference. The light of one firefly triggers those around it until the night is bright with light. Shine as brightly as you can at all times and be the spark that ignites those around you.

October 24

AND FAR GREATER THINGS …

Jesus is the one so many of you worship—and for good reason. He is one who walked upon your earth, cloaked in human vestments, yet one who understood the truth—that man is God with a body. "I and the Father are one," said the Nazarene. But did he not also say, "These things I do and far greater things can you do"? This wise master walked among you to teach the greatest lessons of your life, and still he walks among you.

Use this great master as your model. Can you think of one better? If you were to love all of mankind as you love God, with your heart and soul, judging no one, treating all with equal kindness and compassion, would you then not be as the Father?

Be careful of the metaphors which make the Father into a human image in your mind. Maintain, instead, the quiet knowingness that this loving, ever-present, ever-caring, father-like Force flows within your every cell—aware of you, giving you life. But this Force has no arms, no legs, no eyes, nor ears. For this you are here. Go forth as did Jesus—walking, talking, seeing the world through the eyes of a human, but knowing with no question that you walk as the Father and for the Father, and as such, you cannot fall.

October 25

ON ALLOWING

In order to deal with events which disturb you, recognize that the act of allowing does not mean that you condone all that you observe. It is the same as the act of forgiveness. It both cases, you need neither condone nor agree. By allowing, you are saying, "I see that this reality is unfolding in this way. This is but another expression of Consciousness."

Mankind is gifted with free will to express Consciousness. Oft times, this expression results in that which is less than the qualities of goodness and light. All is part of the Play of Life. By observing darkness, you can better appreciate the light. You, through your choice, can choose to take action or to remain passive, but by allowing Life to play out, you align yourself more closely with the Observer.

Realize that when more than one follow their individual paths of creation, often these paths will conflict. Allow the other paths to twist and turn as they will. You have the choice whether or not to take on a cause—to get involved in paths outside of your own. Always, when you make such a choice, it should be from the heart, with the intention of furthering love.

To allow does not mean that you must always sit back and take no action. It simply means that you recognize that all is simply the Play of Life with all of its dualities. To which end of the spectrum will you lean? Toward the dark or the light? When you do not resist, but allow, you are free to choose.

October 26

NEVER APART

It is in doing nothing
That you accomplish the most,
And not from the achievements
Of which you do boast.

It is the act of non-doing
That makes activity cease,
And there—in not trying—
Do your thoughts you release.

When the mind wants to wander,
It's then you stand still.
You can quiet it not
With the force of your will.

Focus then on the breath—
On the in and out flow…
A movement quite natural,
With no need to blow.

Simply watch as the air
Like the Life Force does move.
This quite simple action
Your calm does improve.

It is there in the silence—
The gap between breathing—
That you find all your thoughts
And your tension are leaving.

For it's when all the thoughts
That do run through your mind
You do finally quiet
That your soul you can find.

Pause each day and do try
Just a while to time spend
And you'll find all your problems
Will begin then to mend.

For deep in the soul
Where pure love does reside
Is the Source of Creation—
Right there, deep inside.

When this place you do visit,
Then you know in your heart
That you and the Creator
Are never apart.

October 27

LOVING INTELLIGENCE

There is a connection between every living thing. You do not need a heartbeat to feel it. Simply look at the beauty of nature: the intricate design of tiny plants, the marvelous physiology of the animal kingdom, the perfection of the human body … Imagine the brilliance of the Mind that designed all of this. Now ask yourself, "Could the same Mind that designed a rose, and a lily, and a shimmering lake, and a beautiful baby not be the essence of love, itself?"

All that is arises from a field of pure potential. Before anything arises, there is nothing but Loving Intelligence. You are a part of that Loving Intelligence. You have sprung from that Source with that intelligent mind and that loving essence as your inheritance. Use these attributes to appreciate the other offspring of the Source that surround you. Touch a flower today and give thanks. Touch a face today and give thanks. Touch someone's soul today and give thanks that you are sharing in this great thing you call Life.

October 28

BELIEF

Belief makes all things possible. When you were a child and you lost a tooth, were not fairies real? When you no longer needed fairies or a white bearded man to bring you gifts, you moved on to believing in other things. What do you believe in now? Do you believe in the innate goodness of mankind, or do you believe mankind is doomed to fail? Your beliefs create reality. Pay attention to what you tell yourself, for these very thoughts shape your world and shape your very body.

When you truly believe that you can do something, that is when you do it. If you cannot do it, dig beneath the surface and look for the word "cannot." Experiment with your God-given power of creation. Play with "can" and "cannot." Once you realize the power you have to create, and the power you have to limit your own creation, then you will begin to move mountains.

October 29

NEVER ALONE

Never fear that you're alone.
It matters not how far from home.
Whether you're around or distant
Of this point we are insistent:

You're always linked within the mind.
Here the connection you will find.
You only think you need the touch,
But this truly matters not so much.

Close your eyes and picture clearly
Those you hold forever dearly.
Can you not create anew
The feelings that they bring to you?

This is the power of the soul
To take two halves and make a whole.
For in the end are ne'er apart
Who once were joined within the heart.

So when you find your steps are weary
And perhaps you're feeling slightly teary
Go within and seek relief.
All it takes is your belief.

Conjure up an image true,
And in your mind will come to you
The vision of the one you miss.
Imagine that you send a kiss.

If this you do, then don't you see
That it's your thoughts that set you free.
For in an instant you create
The love inside for which you wait.

October 30

WHAT IS REALITY?

What is reality? Do you think you have the answer? To you, what is real is that which you perceive. Do your dreams not feel real to you whilst you are dreaming? In that moment, that is your reality. Your dreams elicit emotions just as those in what you call "real life." Hear us now: the waking state is but one level on a very wide spectrum of reality. By broadening your beliefs, you are able to experience more of this spectrum.

Your loved ones who have passed continue to experience reality. Their reality is as real to them as your waking state and your dreams are to you. You normally cannot perceive their reality whilst in the waking state, just as you cannot perceive an x-ray or a micro-wave. This inability to perceive does not mean these other realities do not exist.

There will come a time when you do perceive realities beyond your present one, be it through meditation, a trance state, or the transition you call death. Fear none of these. They merely represent your continued growth and travel along the great spectrum of Life.

October 31

IN THE "NOW"

Look not always toward the future, nor focus on the past. You live only in the present moment. This is all you have. You cause yourself needless worry wondering what will happen days and weeks from now. Realize that you are the creator of "now." As a creator, each "now" that builds upon the other is yours. How do you choose to live in this moment?

When you choose to recognize your true power as a focus of Consciousness and begin to express your true nature as a loving spirit-being, then you begin to experience the perfection of life. As you see your dreams fall into place, then you can relax. With the realization that all is in perfect order always, you know that future now-moments will flow perfectly, without needless worry. You may see the past as now-moments when you were not in the flow. Rather than looking on those moments with regret, see them with loving gratitude for the lessons that they were.

Step into the flow now, and create each now-moment with joy and peace—your true birthrights.

November 1

PRAYERS ARE HEARD

Know that every one of you who walks upon the earth is cradled in the arms of angels. Never are you not cared for or watched over. Know that when one suffers we are at your side, holding your hand. God forsakes no one, for God is the loving Force that animates all living things.

The trials of life are hard for you to bear … the sickness and the surgeries, the suffering, and the pain. The physical body may undergo changes, but know that the spirit is always connected to the Loving Source and cannot be harmed.

When you pray, it is always heard. Your prayers carry a special energy—a loving vibration that is felt and appreciated. Know that the higher good is always fostered by your prayers, even if you cannot see the outward result. Do not cease praying, for this helps all concerned, including yourself. Prayer maintains the link of love, which is always there, but which is strengthened through this most special form of acknowledgment.

November 2

A NEW DAY

Turn the page and begin with a clean sheet. Is this not how you begin each day? Sleep is a time to rejuvenate the body, but also a time to make a clean break from the thoughts and actions of the previous day. The previous day is gone. It exists no more in the light of a new day. What will you create as you open your eyes anew?

Each moment of this new beginning you are given the opportunity to choose how you live your life, how you wish to feel, how you will affect those around you, and how you will allow those around you to affect you. Pay close attention to the latter. Understand that no other affects your moods, your feelings, or your choices. You are the chooser of your moods, your feelings, and of your every action.

Upon opening your eyes each day, spend a moment in gratitude. Then make thc decision to carry that moment with you from moment to moment throughout the day. By living with this attitude, you open your heart to send and receive love, more aware through the expression of gratitude that love is your very nature. Do not waste another day looking at the past nor worrying what will be. Be thankful for this day and all it has to give you. Give from your heart and make the most of this blessed day.

November 3

YOUR PERFECT VESSEL

Bending over, you feel a pain in your back.
What is this? Some kind of attack?
The aches and pains that come with age
Leave you oft with the feeling you're trapped in a cage.

But the body a prison cell is not.
It is, in fact, the best tool you have got.
It's like a pencil in a lesson—
Your very own form of self-expression.

For you are spirit taken form
And with the body's shape you now conform.
It moves in time with your desires
But over time the body it tires.

Look not in anger or disdain
When you feel an ache or pain.
But thank the body for its service,
Even tho' its loss does make you nervous.

To touch and feel and see and smell,
The body thus has served you well.
For as spirit these things you cannot do.
These are the body's gifts to you.

There'll come a day when the body you leave,
And then the truth you will believe.
Then thanks you'll give to what you've felt
With the physical hand that you were dealt.

We hope you see our message clear:
The body you should hold quite dear.
Even if not perfect in the end,
The spirit's tool God did you send.

November 4

FOCUS ON LOVE

Where you place your focus
Is what you do attract.
If you want to find true peace,
You must understand this fact.

You spend so much time watching the news and fretting over the perceived wrongs in your world, and thus you perpetuate them. What would you like to see in your world? Can you imagine if millions of people placed their thoughts on peace and on the well-being of all souls? Can you imagine?

Consciousness creates reality. Your mass consciousness continues to find war and killing acceptable. Were this not so, it would stop. Do not think that you cannot make a difference. Focus on that which you desire to see, not on that which you abhor. In this way you are sending positive vibrations into the vast energy field. These waves intersect with the lower vibrations and cancel them out. Now start a wave of mass consciousness focused on love, kindness, compassion, and respect for life, and be a catalyst for change.

November 5

"SHOULDS"

Should you eat meat? Should you eat meat on Friday? Should you wear a scarf over your head? So many rules, but all of these are merely tools. In the end, the message they send, is which will get you closer to God? You need do nothing to purify the body, but to realize who you are inside: a child of God, pure already.

Your habits will change over a lifetime. Your rituals may evolve. Ask yourself always: What problem do they solve? If by eating less or more, you deepen your connection with God, then stay with the practice. "Whatever works," you say, and this is true. Whatever works to find the real You. Scoff at no other, for each one is your brother. If they dress in different form from what you consider the norm, why do you care? Whatever it takes to get them there.

There are infinite paths to finding God. Some you may find rather odd, but let each man walk his own way. Each will see the light of day eventually, whether here or in the hereafter. For now, may your days be filled with laughter and joy as you enjoy the many paths to Discovery.

November 6

OUT OF THE BOX

You have in your world an expression, "thinking outside of the box." What is this box you have placed yourself inside? It is the box of beliefs which make up your reality. The subconscious mind makes most of your decisions for you from moment to moment based on what beliefs you have previously put in this box. The box can be quite limiting. It is also quite full. Any new ideas you try to place in the box are immediately compared with others already held within. If they do not fit, the ideas in the box rebel and throw out the newcomer.

You can empty the box at any time. We recommend a bit of spring cleaning now and then. Take a look inside the box, and see which thoughts do need to be removed. Replace these with new ones from outside the box that better reflect your soul's constant evolution.

Thinking outside the box is much like accessing your own higher consciousness. In this case, it is your physical body which is the box. Make a shift in consciousness, moving your mind beyond the confines of the brain, and there you will find limitless new ways of looking at the world and at yourself.

November 7

WORK, WORK, WORK

Always there is more work to do. Never can you rest fully in your purpose, but this should not be a chore. The problem lies in your interpretation of "work." Your most critical job in this lifetime is to learn to love. Not all jobs are difficult, and this one should not be so hard, yet do you not make it so at times?

With this understanding of your main task in life, can you not see that you can be working while playing? Can you not see that you can be working whilst sitting in traffic or waiting in a line?

It is not hard to do your work. You are the boss. No one else has supervisory control over your task. You may work overtime or take a break, and there is instant feedback. Give yourself a daily performance review. Do so from minute to minute if things are not going well. "How can I be more loving?" is always the reference point. Choose the path of love in every instant. Be the loving spirit-being that you are and you will find your work a joy.

November 8

BANISH THE DARKNESS

You speak of a devil and give this energy the attributes of an actual being. What is the devil, but the personification of one end of a spectrum of life? At one end you have love, goodness, kindness, and compassion, embodied in a benevolent, fatherly figure. At the other end you have hatred and evil embodied in a man you call Satan.

Neither exists in the form you imagine. Love and hate, goodness and evil are all experiences within Consciousness. You cannot know light until you experience dark. You have no concept of cold without knowing its opposite. Where you place your focus is what you experience. The so-called devil and evil do not exist unless you create them in your mind.

Do you wish to experience only love and goodness? Then place your focus there. These are the true attributes of your Source, for always you are drawn to the higher vibration. The potential for all attributes—good and evil—lie in every man. The choice is always yours what you will experience and express. Be that which you wish to see in the world. Let your light shine so brightly as to banish the darkness.

November 9

VIBRATIONS

Sounds that you hear are naught but vibrations hitting the physical eardrum. Sights that you see are vibrations of light-energy hitting the retina. Things that you touch vibrate at specific frequencies, which the brain interprets as hard or soft. The brain is naught but a grand computer—a frequency analyzer—that gives meaning to the many vibrations which come in through the skin, the ears, the eyes, the nose, and the mouth. But what if you did not have these instruments? Would all cease to be? The answer is no, my friends.

You have come to rely on these sensory inputs, but put these aside and listen with the soul. See with the soul. Feel with the soul. Were you to do so, how your perception of Reality would change! You would understand then that all is vibration, including the soul, and that all vibrates from the consciousness of the Field … your Source … that which you call God.

You are floating in this Field now, held aloft in the arms of Love—the highest vibration. You are sustained with every breath as an experience in Consciousness, for you are that consciousness. Send love and gratitude this day as you awaken to these truths, strange as they may seem. Ask that your eyes and ears be further awakened and simply feel the Love.

November 10

WORD POWER

Your thoughts are the cause of all that you are and have. Your words are your tools. Choose them wisely. A thought expressed in verbal form is manifestation in itself. It carries great power, for it makes the thought more real to you and to those who hear your words, even if the words carry no truth.

Be ever mindful of words which limit you … insidious words like "can't" and "never" which hold the power to limit you from being the all-powerful focus of consciousness that you are. Why do you use such words? Purely out of habit.

Lift the veil of darkness and see these words for what they are: poorly shaped tools which do not reflect your true nature. Shine a light on your vocabulary. Pause before you speak. Ask yourself if the words you are about to utter reflect your True Self and desires, or if they reflect outdated beliefs, self-limiting thoughts, and false perceptions of Reality.

Seek the truth always. It lies within you. As you find it, speak these truths aloud and behold as you reshape your reality.

November 11

A NEW PERSPECTIVE

There is only one Mind at work in your world. Yes, you have your own mind, but just as there are many ever-changing waves in the ocean, there is only one ocean. You understand the analogy, but how does this help you in your daily life as you go about your day?

Once you fully realize and internalize that your mind is a focus of the one Divine Mind, you will look upon your troubles in a wholly—indeed, holy—new light. All challenges are naught but opportunities to tap into that Greater Mind and approach the challenges from that higher perspective.

All of Life gives you choices from moment to moment. If until now your choices have resulted in you being less than your loving best, it was out of ignorance of your true nature. Once you truly understand that nature, making the choice to come from that seat of loving power transforms all troubles and challenges into welcome gifts to express love … only love.

November 12

ALWAYS AT HOME

When you find yourself in some place strange and foreign, do you not at times feel a coldness in the pit of your stomach? These are physical reactions to buried thoughts. If you were to bring the thoughts to the surface, you would find there issues of safety, clouded over with fear. All of these are ancient fears, some carried over many lifetimes.

You are on a path of remembering who you are—a child of God—one who has welled up from the spring of love—your Source. You cannot be separated from this Source, for it is who you are. When you experience fear, this is an indicator that you are focusing on the physical.

What you experience with this coldness is homesickness of the most primal kind. Know that you can go Home in an instant. Simply turn inside to where your Source dwells. Slip back into the warm, inviting waters of your well-source, and bathe yourself in love.

November 13

TRUE BEAUTY

Some things you do "in vain,"
Acting from pure vanity.
You do this without knowing
The thought of separation is insanity.

By thinking of your beauty,
The differences do appear.
"You are more pretty than the next,"
Is what you long to hear.

The beauty's there for all to take,
For Heaven knows no favors.
Surrounded by pure love and light,
Every soul its beauty savors.

But just as on earth there are degrees
Of beauty to behold,
Know that as you learn to love in life,
More Heaven's streets are gold.

November 14

OVERCOMING BLINDNESS

You suffer so from blindness—the inability to see who and what you truly are. Could you but see the radiant light inside, you would never suffer. Why are you so troubled? Why do you cry and treat yourself so badly in word and thought? It is because you are placing your focus exactly where the ego wants you to place it—on the selfish ego. This very real part of yourself keeps itself alive by allowing you to wallow in false thoughts about your true nature.

You are not the caterpillar, but the beautiful butterfly. Allow the butterfly to emerge now and set your spirit free. How do you do this? Shine a light—the very light at the center of your being—on all of the false ego thoughts which you have allowed to have prominence. These thoughts cannot survive in the light of Truth.

Banish the darkness and take flight now. It is never too late, for that is why you are here ... to recognize who you are and let that True Self shine through.

November 15

THIS WONDROUS JOURNEY

You wish to be farther along your spiritual path. Why the impatience? It is because once you have embarked upon this journey of remembrance, the rewards are so great that you become a bit greedy. "I want more of these good feelings," is how you feel. Yes, you feel. That is the point. You feel your spirit awakening, and it is indeed a joyous reunion to be reunited with your Self after a long slumber.

It is true what you have heard, however: The journey is not about the destination. You are traveling into eternity, and thus have nowhere to go. You are exactly in the right place at all times for your soul's growth. Now it is merely a matter of relaxing and enjoying the process of journeying.

It is a paradox, is it not? A journey with no destination other than remembrance. Remembrance of what? That you are spirit … of Spirit. That you are Love, and you exist to grow in your expression of love—your true nature. Can you do that fully in this moment? Yes! And does that not feel most wonderful? No wonder you are enjoying this journey. No wonder.

November 16

FIND PEACE WITHIN

Sit back on your haunches.
Stare up at the sky.
More beauty lies beyond there
Than you can see with just the eye.

The same is true of you, my friend,
If you could only see.
But only when you close the eyes—
It's then that you're set free.

What lies beyond is all illusion.
What's inside is what is true.
What's beyond is ever-changing.
Inside the stillness is pure you.

Change is part of life, you know.
Nothing ever stays the same.
Except the part that gives you life—
The part without a label or a name.

Get to know this part of you,
For it is who you are.
That love-filled space that calls to you …
A subtle longing from afar.

Set aside the doubts you have
That this thing called God exists,
And go within to find It,
To the one whose voice persists.

It's been there calling out for you,
If you would only listen,
And seeking you will find it—
A golden treasure that does glisten.

Grab the gold and run with it,
For this is why you're here—
To find the prize that's yours to take:
Pure Love, without the fear.

November 17

SURFACE AND BREATHE

Surface and breathe. Inhale deeply. With this breath you draw into you the Force which sustains you. Yes, of course it is oxygen which does sustain the body, but it is that which you call the Life Force which does sustain the spirit. The spirit does survive whether or not the physical body breathes, but you can enliven mind, body, and spirit by visualizing the Life Force flowing freely throughout you with each breath.

Do not drown in your sorrows. Inhale deeply. Suck in the Life Force with the intent of bringing unto your Self full vitality and health, both mental and physical. With your mind, send this vital force flowing to wherever there are blockages. Hold the intention of opening these dams and thus returning to balance and harmony.

Surface, breathe, and heal yourself.

November 18

IN THE ARMS OF ANGELS

The death of a loved one is a trying time for those on earth, no matter how enlightened you are. You share memories with the one who passes. You share love and concern. Concern yourself with yourself.

Share with others, and remind yourself that death is a celebration for those who no longer have to bear the pain and darkness of life in the physical world. Know that they are surrounded by love and loved ones who have preceded them. Life will be far easier now for them, and we do stress this word "life," for life is indeed eternal.

Concern yourself far more with remembering the good times, and know that you will share these again. Feel your grief, but do not become swallowed up in it. Allow yourself a period of sadness for the close contact you will miss, then pull yourself back to that place of love within yourself. Do this as a choice. It is not necessary to suffer. Your loved one no longer suffers, and would want you to know this. They look upon you with new eyes and wish you to know that all is well. They are safe and loved in the arms of angels, and so are you, my friend. So are you.

November 19

LOVING VIBRATIONS

Searching, always seeking for the truth
You look beyond.
But the truth lies there inside,
Like ripples on a pond.

Watch the water and you'll see
How the vibrations do spread out—
Energy that moves forever onward.
Your thoughts are like this, have no doubt.

You are pure spirit deep within.
There the purest part it does reside.
And as you thinketh, so you are.
From this truth you cannot hide.

What you think is hidden from your eyes,
But etched forever in your field.
To those who learn to sense the waves,
All is easily revealed.

It is not magic,
Nor to any person should it frighten.
This understanding of your nature
Your spirit will enlighten.

So tune in to these vibrations.
Know that this is who you are.
And more you send out loving thoughts,
More your vibrations travel far.

Expand your Self with loving waves.
In this way, help heal the world.
For with the energy you do project,
The face of God is thus revealed.

November 20

LIKE A SPONGE

All that matters is love. There is nothing else. You are swimming in a sea of love, bathed in it. Your human bodies do act at times like thick wetsuits, preventing you from feeling the love inside you and out. You control how impermeable is this suit.

Discard the thick barrier and become instead as a sponge filled with love ... replete with it. If you could but wring this sponge, it would pour forth onto all around you. This is the goal of life—to realize that love is all there is.

Do not be a dry, brittle sponge, but soak up love until you are sodden, heavy, and bursting. Drip that love on all who come near you, most especially those who thirst. Impart to these thirsty sponges part of your supply, for it is endless. As you give from the Source of your supply, you are endlessly refilled. It is the Law ... the Law of Love.

SOUL SISTERS

There are those who come across your path
Who make you sing and cry and laugh…
Those special souls who touch your heart,
And play a truly special part.

"Soul sisters" you do call these friends.
Your love for them on naught depends.
Their heart and soul you simply cherish.
Without them you'd surely perish.

This is how you feel, at least,
When such a love is thus released—
That God has led you to this one,
Whose light is brighter than the sun.

If you find your sister true,
Cherish what she brings to you,
But know that you do play a role
In brightening your sister's soul.

For this your very paths have crossed—
To find the love that's never lost.
And with this one on whom you rely,
That love inside does multiply.

November 22

SEE WITH THE SOUL

Release all fears. These do block the flow of Life Force like rocks in a stream, causing the current to meander off course at times and to be completely dammed up at others. The Life Force desires only harmony. It will flow where your thoughts go.

What is fear, but the absence of love. If you understood that at the level of the soul you are naught but love, you would know that you have nothing to fear.

The soul is eternal. Troubles, pain, and suffering are part of life in the physical realm. They come and go. The soul is everlasting and changeless. It cannot be harmed. See your troubles and pain as the temporary acting out of thought-energy from the ego, and change your very perception of these troubles. Release the fear. See with the soul and become whole.

November 23

WHEN IN PAIN

Your pain disappears when your wrong-thinking is replaced with love. What is wrong-thinking? Any thought that comes from the belief in separation—that you are anything other than a God-being. You are one with the Creator … one with the loving, creative Force of the Universe. You are the sun and the stars, the wave and the ocean. You cannot separate yourself from love any more than you could separate the breath from the air you breathe.

Wrong-thinking is anything that takes you away from this loving connection with your Source. Fear, hurt, anger, hate, judgment … these are of the ego. These are naught but learning tools and warning signs to you that you are out of alignment in thought. Physical pain occurs when the body is out of alignment. Quite often this misalignment can be traced to misalignment of thought.

Align your thoughts always with love. Love is the great healing force of the universe. Heal yourself with love. It is that simple.

November 24

SIMPLE PLEASURES

Simple pleasures bring a smile to your face: the beauty of a flower … a pair of lovers embracing … the playfulness of a puppy … All of these are so-called mundane sights, yet are they not—in their own way—highlights in your life? This is because they highlight what is most important: beauty, connection, and love.

Did you know that you live for these moments? We do mean this in the most literal sense. You live to experience beauty and love. Do not bypass these moments. Actively seek them out. Pay attention to the world of love and beauty around you as you go about your day. Even in the midst of seeming chaos, these simple pleasures will stand out as if highlighted when you make a concerted effort to look for them. As we said, they are indeed highlighted as the highlights they are. Pay attention and fill your life with pleasure.

November 25

PEARLS

Yes, it is true. Irritants do form the beautiful pearl inside the crusty shell of an oyster. What and who are the irritants in your life? Can you look upon that which grates against you and see that in the grating you are given the opportunity to shine your soul to a brilliant luster?

It matters not how crusty the exterior of your shell. Inside each of you lies a beautiful jewel—the pearl of your existence—your Pure Essence. This expresses itself always as love ... Real Love. There will always be sand in your shell—irritants that cause the ego discomfort. Regard them with neutrality. Send them compassionate love, and shine like the beautiful PEARL that you are: Pure Essence And Real Love.

November 26

GIVING THANKS

On the special day you set aside each year to give thanks, stop and do so for yourself—not just for all the things external. Inside you lies the greatest treasure you can imagine—the link to All That Is. That which you call your True Self is the soul—the part of you which is eternal and eternally loving.

On your holiday you will feast and overstuff the body, but feast as well on love and gratitude. Giving thanks for your very existence brings you into resonance with the Divine and your divine nature.

And so, beloved ones, give thanks not just on your holiday, but on every holy-day of your life. How could each day not be holy when the fact that you exist at all proves your very connection with the Source of all Love?

November 27

THIS TOO SHALL PASS

Focus on the negative. Give all of your attention to that which causes you discomfort. Are you cold, wet, and tired? Wallow in it. Do you mourn and cry from grief? Feel it fully. And now that you have touched this dark side of life in physical form, rejoice, for now you can far better appreciate its opposite—light.

Would you be so uncomfortable when cold, wet, and tired if you had not at one time felt cozy, warm, and fully rested? Would you cry so painfully in mourning had you not at one time opened your heart fully to another and truly experienced love?

"But I want to feel warmth, and comfort, and love all the time!" you cry. And you will, my child, when you shed the physical body and return to the dimension of pure love. But you, yourself, have chosen to take this journey of darkness and light in order to more fully appreciate the light. Light exists in your world, and always it is there inside you when you remove your focus from your temporary miseries. It is then you remember who you are, now and forever.

So wallow for a while, for that is how you learn in this life. But do not wallow for long. Thank the darkness for its teaching … for showing you just how bright light can be. And with this realization, detach yourself from that which takes you farther from the light. Focus no more on the physical and mental discomfort, but sit back as the neutral observer that you are in spirit form and look with compassion upon all events. No matter how you perceive your world, all is sent to you as a gift. Acknowledge each as the opportunity to let your spirit shine through the darkness.

November 28

THE ONLY THING THAT LASTS FOREVER

See not always the danger.
To strife you are no stranger.
But look and see the beauty.
This in life is your main duty.

So very often you deny
That what's before you is a lie.
Nothing is what it does seem,
But pure illusion … like a dream.

This you will finally understand
When you pass completely from this land.
Then the truth you'll finally see:
That you as Spirit are truly free.

At your core, pure consciousness you are.
The part that's neither near nor far,
But always as within just as above …
The seed of God's undying love.

Use this knowledge to find peace.
May it bring you great release
To know your troubles here won't last,
And these too, you will get past.

November 29

THE SYMPHONY OF LIFE

Blessed are those who know the truth … who do not live by the lie of separation. Know ye now that all is one. There is but one vibration, and that is Love. This vibration lies underneath all other harmonies. It creates all the music in the scales. Each of you vibrates in resonance with the One Basic Tone. This resonance becomes discordant when you overlay tones of the ego—the baser vibrations which disguise your core vibration.

Choose discordant thoughts, and your whole experience plays out of tune. Choose loving thoughts, and the music plays beautifully, harmoniously, and well in tune.

You think that this is an analogy, but wait until you shed the physical body with which you now express these notes. Then you will see and hear the basic harmony of the universe … all playing but One Note in a most beautiful symphony.

November 30

RIDE OUT THE STORM

Like a cyclone, problems swirl around you. Do you know what a cyclone is? A force—the movement of energy. Round and round the energy swirls, and what is there at the center, but an area of great calm. You call this the "eye."

Round and round you troubles swarm, but there at your center is the eye of your soul, watching all with everlasting calm. Peaceful and calm are you at your center. When the howling winds rage and the shutters bang noisily, causing you fright and worry, seek shelter there at your center. This is the wise and knowing part of you which knows that the storm will pass and that you are always safe, protected, and loved.

Seek shelter in the eye—the eye of the soul. Become one with the calm. Do not get caught up in the winds and tossed about by them. Sit in the safety of your inner shelter and ride out the rough weather. After the storm, the sun always reappears. Never forget that the true light shines ever brightly within you.

December 1

YOUR SIXTH SENSE

A knocking at the door announces a visitor. You peer cautiously to see who's there. A stranger … one you've never seen before. Do you let him in or does he represent danger? Your stomach clenches. A valid sign. Do not open the lock.

This is intuition—an ever-present source of guidance. Intuition is directly linked to the soul. It is the sixth sense of which you often speak. All of you have this energy sensor. It is part of the True Self. This sense is far more trustworthy than the five physical senses which try to make sense of an illusory world.

Learn to feel without the hands. Learn to see without the eyes. Learn to know with the heart. When danger or opportunity comes knocking at your door, tune in to your soul's sensing system and heed it well. There is far more to this world than the brain will ever tell you. Intuition is a gift of the Spirit. Use it well and wisely.

December 2

ALWAYS CONNECTED

Searching always for answers, you seek outside yourself, but there deep inside you lies the knowledge that you seek. "But how can I know that which I have not been taught?" you ask. It is because you are connected supremely with all that is, all that will be, and all that ever has been. All exists as energy, and as your scientists have proven, energy cannot be destroyed, merely transformed. So transform your beliefs and accept this truth: Thoughts are energy. Every thought that ever has been or ever will be swirls around you and through you now.

With this understanding and the belief that it is so, sit and quiet the mind. The body is your transceiver. Ask to attune to exactly what it is you need to know. Ask your question clearly, then let it go. It will seek its energetic match, and this will resonate with you. Answers are not always instantaneous, so be patient with yourself. This is a new way of thinking and of being connected.

Plug yourself into the grid.

December 3

YOUR BUILT-IN BAROMETER

The eyes water, the mouth yawns, for emotion must escape somehow. When you hold inside you much pressure, it builds and builds. Will it escape in a harsh word or in the striking out of a hand? Or will it not escape at all, but consume your very cells? Recognize when pressure is building. Feel the tension in your muscles. Feel the pressure in your head. Feel the aches and pains … the restlessness. All of these are signs of imbalance and blockage. Is not the body the most perfect messenger?

Listen to the signs. Pay them heed. So many walk in unawareness, ignoring the subtle indicators until they become a glaring billboard. Release your stress through meditation, deep breathing, prayers, exercise, and positive thinking. Recognize that it is your perception and interpretation of events around you which does cause the tightening and the loosening.

The body is a natural barometer. Measure the pressure from moment to moment. You control the release valve … the peace valve. The peace is found there inside—in your perceptions. Perceive the truth that all is temporary but the one everlasting Truth of the Spirit … the underlying Love that rules the Universe.

December 4

BE THE CHANGE

Millennia have passed since the passing of the one you call the Nazarene. He stood as a model to all—a model of peace and loving kindness, and yet still you have wars. Mankind still fails to understand their oneness with each other and with all living things. Do not be discouraged, for focusing on that which disturbs you does perpetuate it. Focus, instead, on that which you wish to see and have in your world. You live in an age of accelerated understanding. Understand that you are part of the change. Be the change you wish to see in the world and add to the acceleration.

Whether or not you call yourself a Christian, all souls can be as the Christ and be the light of the world. You all have it within you—this light—the love that heals all ills and brings others out of darkness. Be that which you are, and bring healing to your world. Focus on the good, and worry not that you make no difference. You make far more difference than you can possibly imagine.

Imagine a world of peace, where all men live as one. It begins with you.

December 5

YOU ARE THE LIGHT

Do you tire of all this talk of love? If so, then why bother to arise from your bed each morning? To learn to live as Love in every moment is your task whilst here on earth and in the hereafter. This task never goes away, nor does the love—merely your expression and experience of it.

Do not wait for love to come to you. Be that which you are … the source of love itself. You need not get out of your bed to find it, for it lies there inside you, whether you lie in a bed or in a bed of roses. If you cannot find this love inside, it is because you have allowed a lifetime of mistaken egoic beliefs of separation and lack to darken your inner light.

It takes not an outside source to turn on the light. You are the light. It burns always there within you. You increase its intensity with your thoughts. It is that simple. Turn up the light and banish the darkness with love, for love and light are the same … and they, my friend, are you.

December 6

DO YOU REMEMBER?

Surrender.
Do not try so hard.
For in the trying,
Your greatest strength you disregard.

It's when you give up all the effort
That you do see great gains.
For in releasing all the struggle,
Naught but love remains.

There is a great Intelligence
That does control the world.
It flows through everything that is,
Like strands of taffy swirled.

They form a grid, these strands of Life.
If only you could see
The web of Love in which you swim—
A shining sea of energy.

This is the Mind of which you're part,
But this you did forget.
Part of the plan agreed upon …
Do you remember yet?

If not, there's yet more work to do
As you uncover Who you are—
A part of this great Life Force
That shares the same light as a star.

As this truth you do remember,
More connected do you feel.
And so you open up the points
And God's true love reveal.

These points of which we speak exist.
They're your connection to the Source.
And with the mind you open them
And allow the energy to course.

So know that you are part of this—
A focus of the Whole.
To understand your place in life,
Just look inside your soul.

December 7

ONE EYE

Never forget who you are. By this we do not mean a person with a name and a title and an occupation with whom you identify so closely. This is not the real you. If you were to remove the words "I" and "my" from your vocabulary, you would begin to have an idea of the real you.

The world appears to be replete with individuals … gatherings of "I's" running around acting on their own, but in Reality there is but one Mind running the show. You are a focus of the consciousness of that Mind. When you fully realize this, your power does not diminish, but increases exponentially. We speak not of power as you know it as an "I," but the power to see the big picture … the power to heal … the power of compassion and love.

See the world through the "eye" of the Great I Am, for this is truly the only "I" that exists … and it is yours.

THE LOVINGEST NUMBER

You have a song in which it is stated that one is the loneliest number. This is a fallacy, when you do come to understand that all is One. There is but one Mind. All of you who feel so alone are but part and parcel of this Mind. And what is this Mind? Is it an impersonal Force which pulls your strings like a puppet and directs your every action? Far from it, dear one.

This Mind is the Source of all love ... the Source of all that is. In order to experience its creative abilities and its magnificence, this loving Source created you. It did create many "you's" so that you would never be alone. Recognize your Self – your godliness – in all whom you encounter. Greet that part of you that is the same—the loving essence which flows through all of life. You are never alone, for never can you be separated from your Source. One is not the loneliest number, but the lovingest number, full of all possibility.

December 9

WHERE HEAVEN RESIDES

Sing the praises of the heavens,
For this very special place
Carries the promise of redemption ...
The way to save the human race.

In this realm of love and light
Exist the angels, true.
And they wish nothing more in life
Than to bring their love to you.

They whisper often in your ear,
Yet you so rarely hear it.
But open up your heart, dear one,
And attune to the world of spirit.

For this is your very birthright—
To make this reconnection ...
To realize from whence you came ...
To have this healing recollection.

And once you do, the love will flow,
And no longer will you suffer.
For all the angels then will come to you
And be a loving buffer.

They'll wrap you in their wings of love,
Protect you from the fate
Of feeling oh so separate,
But please, no longer wait!

Call on them now, these helpers true
Who linger at your side.
Invite them there inside your heart
Where heaven truly does reside.

December 10

UNSEEN HELPERS

The voice you hear in your head you do accept as your own. But we are here to tell you that you are never alone. There is but one Consciousness in the world. Your individual mind is a focus of that one Divine Consciousness. The number of focuses is limitless, but all—while seemingly separate—are connected. How can you separate Consciousness?

Knowing this, we wish you to understand that many of the thoughts you have are placed there for your benefit and guidance by benevolent minds blending with your own. They do this to guide and help you along your path of spiritual growth. Call these unseen helpers what you will: guides, angels, spirit helpers … Give them a name if you wish. It matters not what you call them. When you begin to realize that your thoughts are linked to the One Great Mind, and that you have help along the way, you will call these helpers "friend," and perhaps call upon them more often.

December 11

HEAL THYSELF

Medicines are your way of dealing with illness. They do play quite a helpful role in your world, but do understand they are a palliative measure, and in many cases are not necessary. We do not advise you upon reading these words to cease your medications, merely to understand that you have the ability within the mind to regulate and improve the body.

The body is a reflection of the soul. Imperfections do arise in direct concordance with your thoughts. Yes, a cold is the result of germs circulating in your atmosphere, but you become susceptible to their effects when your thoughts and actions are out of alignment with your true nature. You will find this is true with other dis-eases as well.

Be your own healer. Begin by monitoring not just your physical symptoms, but your thoughts—the very cause of physical symptoms. Healer, heal thyself. You are spirit first and foremost.

December 12

FINDING TRUE LOVE

Many times a couple does get together for the wrong reasons. They are attracted by physical desire. There is nothing wrong with this, but then they do mistake their affection for each other for true love. The love they feel is quite often based on "How can you make me feel better about myself?" While this kind of love is real, it can be temporary, and it most certainly is based on conditions. If these conditions are not met, then you do deem the other unworthy of your love.

True love places no conditions. It matters not how the other behaves, speaks, thinks, or treats you. When you truly love another without conditions, you love that other's True Self--the spirit. And you can only love in this way when you are loving from your own spirit. This is a true soul connection. This love wavers not. If you feel your love for another wavering, then ego is involved, and it is only ego that places demands.

Love from that place inside you that demands nothing, but is the source of all love. There you will find love enough to last a lifetime and into the next.

December 13

TURN UP THE HEAT

Increase the temperature. Keep turning it up, for just as a roast cooks in the oven from the increased heat, you, too, toughen your skin by the same method. Of course we do not mean this literally, but we use this analogy to once again explain that you are forged by fire.

You will face many trials in your life, but you will not know peace until you can look upon the trials as gifts for your soul's growth. You may not have a choice regarding the trials themselves, but always, always do you have a choice as to how you respond to them. Those who do not understand that growth always results from difficulties will suffer greatly. Those who understand the ways of life in a physical body will endure with head held high. They will respond with love in the heart for self-as-spirit, which is awakened by these trials. They will respond with the outward expression of love for all involved in the trials.

In the end, you will see that all are players in the grand drama of life. Your role is not to get caught up in the drama itself, but to remember that you are only playing a temporary role as an actor … an actor, whose true identity is Love.

December 14

LOVE THY BROTHER

Forsake not thy brother in times of trouble.
Be there at his side.
Love thy brother as thyself.
Let him in your heart reside.

Think not of self when others hurt.
Do all you can to aid,
And in this way you help yourself,
For goodness always is repaid.

You scratch one's back, another yours.
In this way all do grow …
Reciprocating love for all
And thus, all God do know.

For God is Love, you've heard this oft,
But know that it is true.
He lives and breathes in others,
Who give their love to you.

If this is so, then know this truth:
You, too, are God in form,
And your True Self you come to know
When loving acts you do perform.

Love thy brother, this we say,
And in this way know God!
For He lies there inside your heart
As that gentle, urging prod.

By giving love you scratch that itch.
The urge you satisfy,
And come to know yourself as this:
God's love, that cannot die.

December 15

BE JOYOUS!

We speak so often of your trials and challenges, but today we speak of joy. Be childlike in your actions and your thoughts. Children know best how to express joy, for they have not yet accepted the false beliefs and negative thought patterns that take you away from being your loving Self.

What is joy, but the celebration of Life itself. Joy is the natural state of the spirit, for the spirit knows itself as pure love. How could you not be joyful knowing this? And so, in this season when you celebrate the birth of one who knew the truths of the spirit, be joyful yourself. Set aside your worries and your cares. Go inside and find the joyful child. Be as the child: smile, laugh, run, and play. Be joyful and alive, then know that this is what Life is truly about.

Life is not the body. The body has a beginning and an end. You, as Spirit here and now, have no beginning and no end. You, as Spirit, are fully alive. Knowing this, rejoice! Share your joy with another today, and see how joy is contagious. Joy does go hand-in-hand with love, and Love is what you are.

CHATTER ON

So many of you complain that you cannot quiet the mind. You wish to sit in the silence, and for this we applaud you. There is no greater way to know your true nature and to commune with your Source. But it is true: You cannot go within and sense your oneness with God whilst the ego is chattering away, trying so very hard to enforce its false sense of separation.

How to overcome this? Quite simple. Begin each period of meditation by chattering away from your heart and soul. You do call this "prayer." Take a few breaths upon sitting with eyes closed, then spend as much time as you need talking to God and your guides and your angels. Share your desires and fears, of course, but most importantly, express your gratitude. Chatter on and on, asking for what you would like to have in your life, and giving thanks that it is on its way.

This period of focused, connected "chatter" will set the stage for the quiet period to follow. In this time of prayer you have made your connection with Your Maker. Now in communion, sit for a moment—or many moments—and simply "be."

Can you think of a better way to spend your time?

December 17

HEADLINES

Where you place your focus is what you do bring into your life. Do you wish to live in a world with more peace and love? Focus on this. Look for this in the world. There are many among you who have not yet realized the power of focused attention. You need not follow the pack.

Your media knows the power of drama and negativity. They are interested in followers, and thus they will continuously put drama and negativity before your eyes. Will you be a slave to their spells, or will you create in your life that which you wish to see?

All is not lost. Around you lies far more goodness than evil, but this does not appear to be the truth if you focus on your so-called headlines. Create your own good news and spread it by radiating love and hope in all directions. "Hear ye, hear ye: The best is yet to come!" should be your headline. Then go forth and create it. Write your own story of love and kindness.

IN TIMES OF TROUBLE

Sitting in a barber's chair to cut your hair …
Do you know who else is there?

The Great Designer … the one who knows
How every hair on your head it grows.

He is the one aware of you now.
To solve all your worries, this one knows how.

Call on Him when troubles you have.
He'll coat your wounds with his loving salve.

He'll hold your hand as alone you walk.
He'll hear your words when alone you do talk.

So call Him now; by your side he does wait.
Share your woes, and all that rests on your plate.

There's no need to think that no one cares.
For it's God who does come as the answer to prayers.

December 19

YOU ARE THAT

God is in your little finger. God fits there.

God is in a mighty oak. God fits there, too.

God is in your every cell. God fills your every hair. God courses through your arteries.

God flows through all of you.

There is nowhere that God is not, for God fills all things. God is not a limited being in a body, nor are you. Once you understand this, you'll find that you can fly. But first you must redefine your conception of "you." You have no fingers and toes, no eyes and a nose. Those are tools the real You is using for a while, thank you very much.

You are just like God, for you are created in God's image. God is what breathes you, fills you, drives you, loves you, is you. You can't get away from God, so stop running so hard. The real You is right there inside, and in your little finger, and in the oak tree, and in everything and everyone you see, because you are that.

Do you get it yet?

December 20

GET OUT AND PLAY

Be as a child; this we say.
Go out this day, have fun, and play.
Too much time you spend inside.
It's as if you want to hide.

But sun and light are good for you.
As is clean grass that's wet with dew.
Get back to nature; get outdoors
Even when the rain it pours.

For this is when you truly see
How it feels to be set free.
This, my friend, is your true state.
So find it now—get out--don't wait!

Take a walk, go on a hike.
Go for a swim, or ride a bike.
Your soul it longs to reconnect
With natural things--this please respect.

For this is where you do belong.
It's God's clean air that keeps you strong.
So while you play, please raise your eyes
And send your thanks toward the skies.

December 21

FIRST CAUSE

To the scientist who believes not in God, we ask him to study his finger. What is it that makes it move and obey his every command? "The brain," he replies. This is understandable, for when the brain no longer functions, the finger no longer functions as well. But what gave rise to the brain in the first place? The brain took form, yes, from the union of egg and sperm. But take that answer as far back as you can go and ask the same question. What gave rise to the first seeds of all that exist? And what keeps all living things living? Why is there life at all? Why is there love?

Deep questions, for sure, and for sure there will always be scientists who can explain away all with reasoned answers. But explain, then, the emptiness experienced inside at the thought of a world created without a loving Creator. Explain away the coldness of a world created not from Love. For this there can be no scientific explanation. For those who have found God within their very hearts and continue to find God by expressing "godliness" through the heart, there is no need for explanations. Experience speaks far more rationally than words or reason.

You may never fully understand the First Cause, but you may come to know it in your heart, and thus banish the coldness and the longing. It is impossible to understand that which is infinite, but fully possible to experience it. Once experienced, there is no need for words.

TRUE RELIGION

Much evil has been done in the name of religion. Unfortunate misinterpretations of the teachings of various masters and abuse of power did lead to the opposite of the true purpose of religion.

People band together to share their joy and love at discovering the truths of the Spirit. In truth, there is no need for a special building in which to do this. There is no need for a leader. There is no need for organizations with rules. There is no need to do anything at all, save for each individual to go within the heart and know themselves as Spirit. The love and joy that comes from this experience will flow forth in such a way that it will beg expression.

Band together to express this, if you will. Be among like-minded souls. Share the love, but be always mindful of the true reason for which you come together: to celebrate the fact that all of you are experiencing the same joy, the same love ... for all of you are of the same Source. Worship Spirit in yourself and others wherever and whenever. Feel the common bond that is Love and express it to one another. That is true religion.

December 23

FRIENDS

Friends are God's gift to you. They teach you a lesson about the ways of life. Why are you attracted to certain people? It is because you share a similar vibration. You resonate together like beautiful notes in harmony. You may not share all interests, but at a certain level you share the same thoughts, beliefs, and emotions. For this reason you emit a similar frequency and are attracted to each other by it.

Together, your spirits sing, and others around you feel it. They are calmed by your presence, for when two or more souls resonate so clearly, others cannot help but be entrained by their loving energy. True friends need not even talk when together, for their energy speaks volumes.

Do you wish to have more friends in your life? Go searching with your heart. Put out your feelers when you come into contact with another. You need not use your eyes or ears ... simply attune to their heart. When your heart sings, you have found a new friend for your orchestra.

Now go create a symphony ...

December 24

IN THIS MOMENT

Each moment of your life you start anew. There is only now. Because of your perception of time, you do see it as a line traveling from a past with a beginning and hurtling forward into some unknown future. We ask you to change your perception. See life from the viewpoint of spirit—which is what you are when not deluded by the body you are carrying around.

How would you see life if you saw only this moment?

Today, look at those you love only in this moment. If you had no past with them, would you love them still? If they had not acted in a way yesterday which did irritate you, would you love them still? If they did not hold the promise of bringing you perceived pleasure tomorrow, would you love them still? See them as they are: equal beings, here to share the here and now. Be still. Be only in this moment, and love them still.

December 25

THE COMMON BOND

You look upon another
And see naught but a face,
Or perhaps a body shape,
Or perhaps the race.

But these are all just markers—
Indicators of a type,
Like the difference 'tween a horse's hair
And a zebra's dark, black stripe.

Inside is where to look, my friend,
To know the person true.
Beyond the face and body,
Each one is just like you.

Be as a blind man—close your eyes
And see all with your heart.
Judge not by what you see outside,
For it's then you feel apart.

See with the spirit—it lies not.
It cuts right to the chase.
It knows that love is what is true,
Beyond the nationality and race.

On this day in which you celebrate
The one who truly knew of love,
Seek to find the common bond
Which Jesus did speak of.

It's God that does unite you,
For as God you were created.
And His kingdom lies within you,
As His son so clearly stated.

Celebrate his birth with happiness
And joy forever more.
Judge not, but love as Jesus did
And from God's cup the love will pour.

December 26

VIGILANCE

There are many strains of viruses,
All caused by different germs,
And each does harm the healthy cells
In no uncertain terms.

Your thoughts are like these illnesses.
They attack what's well and good.
You'd see they're quite insidious
If see your thoughts you could.

And so you must be vigilant
And not let your thoughts run wild.
With firm hand you must control them,
As a caring parent with its child.

The analogy's a good one
For like a child thoughts do grow.
And if left alone and uncontrolled
Then true chaos you do know.

But given love and guided
Good thoughts inside do bloom.
Instead of causing pain and strife
They heal, thus given room.

While germs and sickness run amok
Your thoughts you do control.
So monitor what's in your mind
Before these germs do take their toll.

Should pessimism be the norm
Of how you think each day,
Replace your thoughts with love and light,
And heal yourself this way.

December 27

WHEN YOU GRIEVE

One you know has passed from the physical body. They no longer breathe the same air as you, but are you not aware of them in your thoughts? "Yes, but this is just a memory," you say, " … a figment of the imagination." And while this is true, do you not in this way keep them alive in your consciousness? We wish you to understand that all you see and experience is naught but consciousness. Do you know that you cannot trust the physical senses? These do mislead you. That which you create with consciousness is as real as that which you see.

There will come a time when you, too, pass from the physical body. Then you will see again those who have passed before you. But you will not see them through physical eyes. You will see and know them through consciousness, which is all that exists. Keep them alive for now in your thoughts, knowing that they live still, but in another form of consciousness. Your body prevents you from sensing them unless trained to transcend the body. For now, use the power of consciousness to bring them alive in your mind, and do know that in their current state of consciousness they are quite aware of you.

The physical body does die, but consciousness is eternal. You are that, and all that you see is that. Hold onto that when you grieve, then grieve no more.

December 28

THE SPACES IN BETWEEN

It is in the silence that you should delight. Your lives are filled with noise. What is noise, but the outward manifestation of vibration. What is vibration, but the creative manifestation of God—the Absolute, the non-vibrating First Cause. Noise, just as all vibration, carries information. But you can be overloaded with information. How much do you need to take in at any one time? There can be too much of a good thing.

Silence is golden. All arises from this. You could not appreciate the beautiful notes of a symphony, save for the silence between each note. You cannot truly appreciate the beauty that is Life, unless you stop and listen carefully to the silence between the beats of your life.

Create silence in your day deliberately. In those moments when no noise floods your ears, it is then that you will hear the true voice of God. It is then you realize that you and all that is have arisen from this silence and to this silence you will return. Be ever grateful for the silence, and then return to the world of manifestation and make a beautiful noise. Express love with your voice, with your hands, with your eyes, and with your heart and soul, and then you, too, will know what it is like to be a creator.

December 29

FEAR NOT

It is all very simple, this thing you call life, yet you make it so difficult. There is love and there is fear. That is all. Everything you do is a choice between the two. How hard is it to choose love? It only becomes hard when you let your lower self get in the way. This is the part of you that acts in self-protection and self-promotion. In other words, the part that acts from a place of fear. "Fear of what?" you ask. Fear of not having or getting enough love. Fear of being hurt. Fear of dying.

All of these are attributes endured by the physical body, where nothing lasts. You are far more than the physical body. You are formless, limitless spirit, temporarily using that body you call "yours." You are not temporary. You are eternal, just as love is. Fear is temporary. Lack is temporary. Love is everlasting, and there is no end to its supply. You can endure anything, knowing it is temporary. This too shall pass. This too shall pass. But love does not pass by. Love is ever-present and there for the taking … there inside of you and in everything you see. Reach out and take it. Better yet, give it. It is there for you to give always, for as spirit, love is your very essence.

December 30

DIVE IN

In an effort to be and see only goodness, do not shut out the outer world. Yes, it is true: There beyond the Self is a world of duality—of good and evil, love and fear. This is why you are having this earth-bound experience: to learn from the differences.

Once you taste the sweetness of living as a conscious spirit-being in human form, you will want nothing but this experience of bliss. But hear us now: You are here for the full experience of life. More bliss awaits, but in the meantime, dive in and live fully. Do not run from the darkness. Do not hide or seek shelter when you feel the baser vibrations around you closing in. Merely step back a bit, observe with detached compassion, and send love. In this way you are a full participant in the healing process—both of your world and of your soul.

There is no need to live in a cave or in a self-made bubble of happiness. That safe place always lies within. Go there as needed, but be fully present in the play of life.

December 31

HIGHER AND HIGHER

You say that you are attempting to contact higher aspects of yourself. And then the doubt does creep in. "How can there be anything but this self that I know as 'me'?" For a lifetime you have placed your focus on "me," and it is this very myopia which has led to the blindness of so many. Take off your blindfold now and expand your focus. Shift your consciousness to a reality far more grand than a small blue marble which floats through the cosmos. Put on new lenses which allow you to see a reality of multiple dimensions in which the greater part of you wanders, explores, and connects with all of Life.

Have we not told you that all is One? If that is so, then the lower self you know as "me" is "one" with a higher self and all selves. Do you get it yet? When you connect with your higher self, you are tapping into the One. The One is fragmented into you, and your neighbor, and your cat, and a rose. But this is just one level of All That Is. Why would not the One be fragmented into spirit guides, angels, and distant galaxies unseen by the human eye at a level beyond which you now place your focus?

Place your focus on infinite possibilities. It is quite a wondrous world you inhabit, but it is only one world. Take off your blindfold and set yourself free.